Essential Guide To Public Speaking For Beginners

A Handbook To The Art Of Public Speaking: The Do's And Don'ts

Alice Dean

© Copyright 2020 - All rights reserved.

The content contained within this book may not be reproduced, duplicated or transmitted without direct written permission from the author or the publisher.

Under no circumstances will any blame or legal responsibility be held against the publisher, or author, for any damages, reparation, or monetary loss due to the information contained within this book, either directly or indirectly.

Legal Notice:

This book is copyright protected. It is only for personal use. You cannot amend, distribute, sell, use, quote or paraphrase any part, or the content within this book, without the consent of the author or publisher.

Disclaimer Notice:

Please note the information contained within this document is for educational and entertainment purposes only. All effort has been executed to present accurate, up to date, reliable, complete information. No warranties of any kind are declared or implied. Readers acknowledge that the author is not engaged in the rendering of legal, financial, medical or professional advice. The content within this book has been derived from various sources. Please consult a licensed professional before attempting any techniques outlined in this book.

By reading this document, the reader agrees that under no circumstances is the author responsible for any losses, direct or indirect, that are incurred as a result of the use of the information contained within this document, including, but not limited to, errors, omissions, or inaccuracies.

Table of Contents

Introduction
    Adopt Characteristics For Success
Chapter 1: Anxiety
    Facing It
    Coping Skills
Chapter 2: Verbal Communication
    Pitch
    Intonation
    Volume
    Energy
    Pauses
    Pronunciation
    Dialect
    Articulation
Chapter 3: Non-Verbal Communication
    Body Language
    Eye Contact
    Movement
    Appearance
Chapter 4: Common Mistakes
    What Are They?
    How To Avoid Them
Chapter 5: Your Speech
    Different Speeches
    Getting Messages Across In Different Types of Speeches
    Controlling The Room
    Having Self-Confidence
    How To Write A Good Speech

    Visuals

    Length Of The Speech

    The Beginning

    The Body

    The Ending

Chapter 6: The Audience

    Analyzing Your Audience

Chapter 7: Speech Versus Communication

Chapter 8: Improving Memory

Chapter 9: Reading Your Speech

    How To Deliver Your Prepared Speech

Chapter 10: Preparing For The Q&A Section

Conclusion

References

Introduction

"Stress, don't get me down."

"Don't you dare overthink."

"Perhaps I can't do this..."

Yes, you absolutely can! Just like everybody else who did it before you, especially anyone who has struggled to speak in front of people, and believe me, you are not the only one. Whether you find it difficult to speak in front of a crowd or preparing something to present that could potentially go all wrong, there are quite a few reasons why people don't want to get up on a stage and speak their minds like many want to. Sometimes, it's not so much that people are afraid of humiliation or not being prepared enough, which believe me, is the primary cause of struggling to present yourself on a stage but it's also because everybody has a unique personality. The one person is not the same the next, yet with this, we can still group people according to their personality traits.

Take shy people, for example. They are faced with an entirely different set of challenges than people who are confident and don't even feel a rush of adrenaline when they get up on stage and speak what they've prepared–sometimes not even prepared, on a stage.

Public speaking is like a skill, and unfortunately, not everybody feels like they can become proficient in it. And, while this may feel true at the moment you are counting down your queue to do what you came or are expected to do, what many people don't realize is that any skill can be learned if you persevere to try. With that belief in mind, overcoming any fears associated with potentially being embarrassed, judged by others– especially your peers, or falling into the thought of not doing good enough, are all things you need to get past. Think of fear as a mental barrier. It's a tunnel you have to dig through, and while some people's tunnels are deeper than others, everybody has their own set of things that they need to work on to become a better version of themselves, whatever their occupation or purpose may be. Everybody struggles with something, and because humans are in constant need to learn, there is comfort in the fact that you, like everyone else, are a work in progress. If you think about the most successful public speaker you know, consider this... They had to start somewhere, and you can bet one-hundred dollars on it that they did not feel comfortable or at their best when they had to deliver their very first speech.

If you ask me what you could do to become better and always be at your best, my advice to you would be to prepare as much as you can, become disciplined, and find a way to deal with whichever fear you live within your mind, but still, it will be what you make of it. Thinking about public speaking, you should keep in mind that a person who speaks and stutters during his or her speech, but finishes, is more successful than the person who doesn't try at all or makes excuses why they can't deliver a speech. The same goes for everything else we do in life. The person who shows up and delivers the best they can, regardless of their competencies or skills is likely to be more respected and successful in all they do than the person who believed they were too perfectionistic or scared to encounter potential mistakes.

Don't get me wrong, public speaking is challenging. It's one of those things that you either feel good or bad about and usually, many people hate it. However, looking past all the things that could go wrong or why you don't like speaking in front of others, there are valid reasons why public speaking is crucial in society, including the institutions we find ourselves in.

Public speaking is significant in education, politics, business, and in the face of the public in all settings. If you have a platform to speak on, you are a public speaker–no matter where you are–particularly if you are addressing something important to a lot of people. The fact that you could impact a crowd is not only incredible, but it's relatively powerful, and it's also something that people take for granted. If you think about the world we live in today, countless issues are either not addressed, misrepresented, or not talked about enough. When you add your voice to the mix, you get to decide what people will hear, whether it's at school during a speech, a business meeting to present an idea, or a politician, perhaps even a philanthropist, trying to add their two cents to change the world.

With that being said, don't you see? Can't you imagine? You can be anything you want. Yes, you are one voice, but know that the world can use your voice. No matter what language you speak, you can be heard. The world can gain value from your opinion and perhaps even draw inspiration and hope from your words. It can ignite a flame in others to do the same, and address or add awareness to causes and situations you believe in. It is crucial for everybody–every generation, but specifically the younger generation. Generation X and millennials are the two generations responsible for the future, and all that we have to start a conversation about or continue to talk of now. It includes climate change, world peace, fair politics, gender-based violence, corruption, necessary action on injustice, which have been highlighted in recent years already, yet isn't close to being resolved, among many other things. Oh, and don't forget about human rights–something impaired in too many ways today, from lacking access to clean water to children dying of hunger, freedom of speech, equality, and let's not even start to talk about existing slavery in the 21st century.

When you approach public speaking, you are representing something bigger than yourself. Keep that in mind that perhaps it will give you the power to get through.

Look at it as a presentation in front of a live audience that could bring value to more people than just yourself, because that is what it is. In a way, it's a selfless act to speak about things that should be heard. Apart from general speeches that can encompass just about anything, public speaking is impactful as it focuses on a goal to educate and influence people at large, sometimes even entertain them. As a part of public speaking, you know that a speech is the number one source used to relay information to a public setting of people, but so are electronic slideshows and visual aids, both of which are used to supplement a speech to keep an audience intrigued. These sources are helpful to steer attention in the technologically advanced age, or should we say, disabled age, which tends to be more focused on a screen than any pressing issue or cause at hand.

Today, we are forced to make use of online presentations, sometimes more than physical public speeches, which is why understanding how to use visuals to your advantage, is necessary to deliver a successful speech. Online presentations are still delivered to anywhere between a few to many people but are more flexible. When you start out speaking in front of people, it is helpful to first start by practicing speaking in front of people online. With the help of a video, you will have less pressure to perform optimally. The setting is informal, which may put you more at ease than a public setting.

When you get the opportunity to speak in front of an audience, keep in mind that there is plenty for both you and them to learn. They are taking the time to listen to you speak your mind and narrate your opinion, which is surreal if you think about it. When you get the opportunity to do this, you have a voice. Regardless of how confident you feel, or how inadequate, know that it is in your hands to deliver something useful. By thinking of a public speech like this, instead of a stressful event that will likely make you feel bad or embarrassed about yourself, is a fixed manner of thinking. It does not matter how much you doubt yourself. If you want to evolve, you can choose to grow instead of remaining in your comfort zone or stuck in your head where you've probably been for a long time. Even if you fail, you can say that you've grown, which is more than the person who didn't try could ever say.

By trying more often, you will learn how to let go and start doing it. Eventually, you will not ponder on the consideration of whether you can or can't do something. You'll be a doer instead of a quitter, which can aid in your confidence, strengthen deductive skills, empower you, improve research skills, and provide you with the ability to advocate significant causes. Of course, this can only be done by working on yourself, including your skills, improving until you become comfortable with presenting yourself and speaking your heart out to the world. In this guide, you will learn to do just that and more, so let's explore.

Adopt Characteristics For Success

- Confidence.

    It is not easy to be confident, and those who are naturally confident are truly blessed beyond comparison. However, since working on your skill to become a sensational public speaker is all about growth, you must learn how to be confident. It's okay if you didn't step out of the womb with a strut in your step, but now is your chance to shine, even if you like to dim your lights. To be confident, you must be accurate, credible, appear intelligent, knowledgeable, competent, believable, and likable. This may seem like a tall order to fulfill, but if you can take confidence and break it down into these factors, you can start learning how to improve each one, one at a time.

    Keep in mind that, no matter how confident someone appears to be, they are still nervous, they are just good at hiding it, which means they basically present themselves as liars in broad daylight. Remember that.

    When you are in fear, instead of basking in it, replace it with excitement. You can trick your mind in believing you are excited rather than scared or nervous. When you focus on this idea, you will feel more comfortable in front of others.

- Passion.

    To communicate with the people who are taking time out of their schedules to watch you and learn what you have to say, you have to speak with passion. If you don't, your speech will be nothing but meaningless. With that, displaying sincerity is a good way to communicate with your audience. If you intend to leave an impression on your audience, you must mean what you say. If you don't believe in your work and what you are sharing with others, you will likely lose their attention early in your speech. To speak with passion, you also need to know who it is you are communicating to. By studying your audience, you will have a better idea of what to say to them and how to say it. If the topic interests you, you will speak with enough passion to intrigue the people who are listening to you.

- Authenticity.

    When you deliver a speech in front of people, and the attention is on you alone, it's natural that you will feel stressed. Everybody experiences it to some extent. What separates a person who performs regardless and one that struggles is learning how to deal with it effectively. If your personality contributes to your stress or isn't comfortable in front of a large group of people, the last thing you should do is think that there is something wrong with you or that you have to change. Being yourself is the best thing you can do if you are trying to connect to your audience. It doesn't matter how formal your speech or presentation is, you still want your audience to be engaged, which can only be done if you let loose and personalize the experience for everybody. If you write a speech down and study it to the final word, only to deliver it like you are reading a photocopy thereof in your mind, you are likely to bore your audience. If you want to gain their attention and leave a bigger impact, you must be yourself. Trying to be someone you are not will only make you more nervous, as you now also have to focus on being what you are not. In that same breath, don't memorize your speech. You are not a robot. Highlight important points and talk to your audience to keep them interested in what you have to say. With being authentic, be sure to always stay true to yourself and what you believe in.

- Preparation.

As one of the most significant steps in public speaking, you can't do anything without preparation. It should be taken seriously. Sometimes, with any project, it seems impossible to start, especially with a challenging project that presents a new initiative to you. If you don't know a topic or how to do something, what would you do?

You will research to understand and prepare the layout of information you need to process or simplify into a presentable manner. Without preparation, you can't start to write your speech or create your presentation. If you only have a topic, you won't know what to write, who you are talking to, how to provide value to your audience, or how to execute a stellar speech. It should all be taken into consideration when you prepare your speech. With adequate research, you can prepare, and with that, feel more confident about what you are going to say to your audience. When you study a topic, you can also give yourself time to personalize it and derive your own opinion about it, which will simplify your speech, along with the delivery thereof.

- Voice modulations.

When you deliver a speech, you can't do so with one tone of voice. You have to change your tone regularly to keep your audience engaged. If you have one tone, you will seem like you are too well-rehearsed, almost like you are reading your speech from a piece of paper. To deliver your speech effectively and keep your audience interested, you will have to practice it without over-rehearsing it. The point is not to be perfect with practicing your speech. The point is merely to become comfortable with the topic, almost to become conversational about it.

The more you practice, the more inauthentic you will sound, which is why you need to pay attention to the tone of your voice. It also doesn't matter who your audience is. It doesn't matter whether they are a different nationality, for instance, you should keep your voice and accent the same. Don't focus on sounding too professional either. Just go with your natural voice.

- Keep to the point.

To say that you should keep it short and sweet is great advice, and you should take it if you can. But, what if you can't? What if you are requested to speak for a set amount of time, say 30 to 60 minutes? Well, then you will have to break down your speech into sections to keep your audience engaged. If it is possible, keep your speech as short as you can, as this will keep your audience more engaged and locked in on what you have to say. When you prepare your speech, remove all the unnecessary information you possibly can. Keep it to the point and consider whether what you are writing has any relevance or value to your audience. If it doesn't, don't talk about it. If you know that what you are about to share with your audience is valuable to them, it will also seem much easier to deliver your speech with confidence. When you are presented with a long duration to fill your speech in, keep it short, and make time for a Q & A section, which will be more helpful to your audience than sometimes, the speech itself.

- Tell a story.

Paint a picture with the help of storytelling. It will aid in your speech by making it more interesting, impactful, and for you, easier to convey. If you think about yourself, you wouldn't want to sit through an hour-long speech that is boring and repetitive, or filled with information that doesn't have any relevance to you. When you speak with creativity and without being too serious, you have a greater chance of success in delivering a speech. It will add energy to the atmosphere around you, increase awareness of the target audience, and allow you to try various non-verbal communication gestures. It will also help you work on your body language to improve your speech altogether and provide an entertaining space for you to make jokes or poke fun at yourself. Reviewing other successful speakers, you will find that all of them are likely to use storytelling to their advantage. It is a skill you can learn and use as a powerful tool to connect with your audience.

- Focus on repetition.

If you want to use your platform to teach others self-help tips or take away keynotes, you can repeat sections or ideas that you want them to focus on. It can be quite helpful in writing a speech if you focus on the goal thereof–something you want the audience to remember or think about once you are done with your speech. You could always focus on such a goal or concept, and then focus your Q and A section around the main point of the speech, for the audience to gain more insight, opinions, and mental clarity about what you are trying to teach them. If it is long, repeating parts you want them to focus on is helpful to achieve the point of your speech.

- Be a human about it.

When you are writing your speech, focus on what your audience needs to hear, and not just what you think they want to hear. You don't want them to enjoy your speech. You want them to learn from it. If you have a platform to speak on, you should use it wisely and remember that just like you, the people who are watching you speak are continuing to learn too. In essence, they are learning on the go as you are, and with this idea in mind, you don't have to be worried about making mistakes or delivering an opinion that doesn't dance to everyone's song. Everybody is human. We are all a part of the same species. We all have opinions, and we also feel fear, anxiety, and stress in the same way–even if one feels it more or less intensely than the other.

Chapter 1: Anxiety

To speak publicly is a real fearful event unless you learn how to deal with it effectively. The fear of public speaking is not a thing you can get over with the snap of your fingers. Some people live in fear of it to such an extent that it holds them back from getting ahead in their career or expressing the things they want to share with the world. It is common among different forms of anxiety. It is almost as derailing to your mental health as a physical illness is to your body, and could range from slight nervousness to experiencing complete paralyzing panic and fear. Basically, it rules your life. It can be indicated by the way a person presents themselves when they are placed on the spot, having to deliver a presentation or speech. Someone who doesn't have a fear for public speaking won't go out of their way to avoid it, just like with a social setting or invitation, whereas a person who is fearful of it will do everything to not speak in front of others or avoid it. It is especially the case when presented with stressful situations that increase anxiety. When one is nervous it can be detected by others. Do you know that saying about smelling fear? Well, there is some truth to it. People can see when you are scared by paying attention to the tone of your voice, usually a quivering tone in combination with a bad posture or shaking hands. Some people get so nervous that they start to sweat, while others experience headaches or blackout and faint.

Anxiety is an awful thing. It's not your friend, and it has a way of negatively affecting many parts of your life, especially your career and personal or social life. It can have a massive impact on your ability to perform and can hold you back from getting a promotion or delivering the best version of yourself that you know you are, but struggle to show. It is debilitating and frustrating. Many who experience anxiety feel out of control, and like they can't get over it, but what many fail to realize is that it is a process that requires work.

It is one of the leading causes why people fail to do what is expected of them and are held back in the things they want to do. Believe it or not, it is considered so bad that it ranks as the most common phobia next to death, heights, and spiders, which seems irrational, but shows you how serious it can be.

Anxiety in public speaking is medically known as glossophobia. It's not something made. It's a mentally-altering condition that affects nearly 73% of the U.S. population, which mostly occurs as a result of fearing judgment or the negative evaluation by those who are watching. Public speaking is a literal anxiety disorder. The seriousness thereof can often be misunderstood and cannot be emphasized enough. The people who experience it tend to feel hopeless and like nothing can help them overcome it. Today, however, where answers are made readily available everywhere, it is quite upsetting, if you are not able to present yourself in front of others professionally, confidently. (National Social Anxiety Disorder, 2016)

Speaking in front of an audience makes us feel vulnerable to rejection, which for many people, is one of the scariest things they could experience. People hate rejection and avoid it as far as they can because nobody wants to feel like they are not welcome, wanted, or accepted. Perhaps one of the biggest fears of public speaking that is related to anxiety is brain freeze, which is the prospect of gaining attention from your audience, only to stare them on in silence with the feeling of judgment or rejection. Brain freeze is, unfortunately, common among people with anxiety. It affects the brain's prefrontal lobes that are responsible for memories. They are also very sensitive to anxiety and can get triggered quickly. When your brain experiences brain freeze, you become more stressed, which increases your stress hormone and shuts down your frontal lobe. It also disconnects from other parts of your brain, which makes it even more difficult to retrieve memories.

Since your body experiences a very high level of stress, it activates your fight or flight response—an indicative threat to your safety that requires action immediately. When we are delivering a presentation or speech, and this occurs, you can imagine how the brain doesn't know what to do. All that it gets told is that it has to get us to safety, and when we are on stage, it disrupts our ability to function. Although speaking to the people in front of you isn't life-threatening, your prefrontal lobes can't distinguish between what's real and what's not, so it responds without giving you the option to think first.

Public speaking can be hidden by choosing your career wisely. If you were a kid or college student in school, it's possible that you didn't have a choice but to conduct speeches in front of a class or audience regularly. However, with your career, if you picked one suited for you, you probably don't have to deal with it. Countless people who do, and some struggle to speak up in a group or raise their voice in meetings, which is similar to experiencing anxiety with public speaking. In either of these cases, you can address it. The key is to keep your brain alert to danger, but the right type of danger, instead of something you are insecure about or afraid of based on your feelings or personality traits. In truth, nothing is as bad as it seems. You have to convince your mind about that. To overcome anxiety for speaking up or speaking in front of others. You must change your response to excessive fear or stress, which can be done in a few ways.

Facing It

- De-catastrophize brain freezes.

    When you experience brain freeze, it's a terrible thing that makes you feel like you want to dig yourself a deep hole and hide in it. It's the feeling of being embarrassed that nobody wants to feel, and at times, it doesn't matter how much you prepare to do good in something, there are times that you will disconnect and struggle to speak the words that you wanted to. Imagine being asked a question and knowing the answer, but because you are faced with too much stress, you try to answer it as briefly as you can. It may make you seem like you are not interested, informed, or unprepared, even if you are overprepared. When you get a brain freeze in front of a big audience, you can do one of two things. You can either be affected and focus on it so much that you are thrown off your game, or let it pass, forget about it and continue your speech, interview, or whatever situation it is you find yourself in. What you have to remember is that the moment you freeze up will have been forgotten as you return to normal to deliver your speech, so worrying about it is not helpful to you or your audience.

- Forget about being perfect.

    You can only overcome fear, or whatever is holding you back from speaking comfortably in front of others, by setting achievable standards for yourself. Perfectionism is a personality trait that has been viewed in both a positive and negative light. People beat themselves up about not being perfect, while others strive to perfectionism. There's nothing wrong with wanting to be better at what you do or want to do. The problem is setting expectations for yourself that you can't meet. It usually sets you up for failure mentally, because if you set the bar too high, it's very likely you won't achieve what you want. With writing and delivering a speech, you should know that it will never be perfect and that anything can happen regardless of how much planning you do. What you should also remain aware of is that you will have many kinds of personalities in your audience. You will have no way of knowing what they are, how people's opinions are, or how they will respond to what you say. With this, you can rest assured that it doesn't matter if you aren't perfect. Sometimes, the flaws you show is what makes your speech relatable and unique. It should make you feel comfortable, at least.

- Choose silence.

    Sometimes, we talk too much. It's something we are too fixated on, instead of listening. It is an interesting concept for introverts versus extrovert personalities. You are either one or the other, if not a combination of both. Being extroverted, you are likely to be talkative, outgoing, and outspoken. If you are extroverted or lean more towards it than being introverted, you are likely to fill all the silence you can with conversation and share your thoughts and feelings. However, the opposite is true for an introverted person. In this case, extroverted personalities are recommended to take it down a notch. A person that talks all the time can learn from being quiet every once in a while. It will be beneficial for them to practice being more silent during conversations with others. The point of this exercise is not to make you talk less because talking a lot is a bad thing. The takeaway from it should be to become more comfortable with silence. Introverts don't have a problem with pauses so, regardless of the challenges they may face delivering a speech, they have the upper hand in being comfortable with stopping without thinking of a pause like something uncomfortable. It is a good way to work on your ability to face various challenges during your speech that you may have been unaware of before. It will make your speech go smoothly.

- Leave it there.

When anything bad happens during your speech, you can choose to pay attention to it or leave it. Although an awkward moment on stage or whatever platform you are on may seem distracting to you or your audience, focusing on it even for a second too long is probably the worst thing you can do. Instead of doing this, leave it. You can learn from it after your speech and avoid making the same mistake in the speeches you are yet to deliver in the future. Instead of small moments getting you down, focus on the bigger picture, which is that you are in control of the entire speech or presentation you are delivering. When you think of it like this, you can turn even the smallest mistakes into an opportunity to create a more positive memory.

- Practice presentation flow.

Delivering a speech is not about how precise you are in the moment. It's more about being intune with your audience, which can only be done by maintaining a proper presentation flow. When you practice your speech, you mustn't over practice it. If you do, you may start focusing on your errors, rather than on how your audience is receiving and interpreting your message. One of the best things you can do is put yourself in your audience's shoes. How would you feel about the speech you are delivering if it was you listening to someone else speak? Would you gain value or a helpful and resourceful take away from it? Or, will you forget about it once it's over? To make an impact, you must focus on how you make people feel. Your presentation should be like a puzzle you piece together from the start to the end of your speech.

- Always be prepared.

Imagine if you were prepared for anything–every downfall or mishap. You would be one of the most in-control people in the room, wouldn't you? The trick with being prepared is to not take it too seriously, while at the same time being precise about what you are preparing for. If you know that you need to practice your speech a couple more times, do it. If you know that it will help you to practice it in front of others, do it. The same goes for everything else. Spend quality time on learning how to deliver your speech and consider what could go wrong. For instance, if you know there is a part you struggle to convey, find a way to do it better, or change the subject if you do encounter the struggle during your speech. Being prepared also prepares you if something does go wrong when you are delivering your two cents to an audience. By teaching yourself to remain calm, you can endure anything with ease and recover from it just as easily.

- Breathe.

I don't have to tell you how essential mindful breathing is. It's pretty helpful, especially when you want to reduce anxiety. It can be done by taking breaths by slowly inhaling and exhaling at the same pace. You should consider pausing in between breaths to ensure you are indeed in control of them. You can practice this connection when your stress levels are low, and your mind is at ease. Don't start practicing on the day of your speech. Give yourself time to form a mindful breathing mind-body connection that you can implement in high-stress situations.

- Speak at a glacial pace.

When you are nervous, the number one thing you may want to do is speed through your speech, but that's probably the worst thing you can do. There's no way rushing your speech or presentation will make you feel good, deliver the right message to your audience, or even leave the impact you intend to make on them. Besides, the faster you go, the more likely you are to make mistakes, and in this case, ones you won't necessarily be able to recover from. Practice speaking slowly and clearly, rather than forcing too much information into your speech. The brain considers speaking fast as a threat, so speak slowly to calm your mind to send relaxed messages to your brain.

- Don't stare at the wall.

At school, we are taught to, if you feel like you are under pressure, find one point in the class and stare at it while you deliver your speech. However, this is the worst thing you could do. That means you have been taught wrong. You should make contact with your audience and connect with them instead of avoiding making eye contact. By making deliberate eye contact with your audience, the people you are talking to will feel like you mean what you are saying and find you more genuine or worth listening to. On the flip side, your confidence will increase as seeing that people are interested in what you have to say can aid in maintaining your composure and push you to do your best.

- Find a support group.

    If you have a lot of anxiety or succumb to stress too easily, you should find a group of people that can make you feel comfortable. By repetitively exposing yourself to situations that are perceived uncomfortable by you, eventually, your brain will change the way it thinks about the situations you were initially afraid of. It will help you improve your ability to speak to a large group of people and allow you to cope with your fear successfully. By getting comfortable in a group setting, you will feel more relaxed about taking on challenges in public speaking, which can push you to grow.

Coping Skills

Communicating speech can be very easy or very stressful. For most people, it's one of the most challenging things to do. Keep in mind that this is not everybody, but everyone to some extent, requires inspiration, motivation, or strategies, to keep them going when the barrier in their mind tells them that they can't do it. Communication is presented in different forms, and we should all do our best to try and become efficient in these forms. Since talking is the communication form that we use the most, working on our ability to talk flawlessly is one of the best things we can do for ourselves. See, public speaking is a skill that you need to learn, but so is talking, in general. Sure, you may not feel like it is necessary, but are you doing the best you can? People can always highlight whether you are performing well or not. They can tell you to speak up, repeat yourself, be clearer, elaborate, etc. At the end of the day, you are the one that needs to see where you are struggling and address it accordingly. If you can notice your challenges, you can address them, but if you can't be honest with yourself and point them out, they will remain. They could even possibly get worse or become more difficult to deal with overtime. Your inability to communicate effectively can hold you back. It can keep you from taking chances in your career and thriving as you should.

7 Elements of public speaking to cope with challenges:

1. Speaker.

You are the speaker, and if you are not, take note of those who are. If you want to improve, one of the biggest ways to do so is to learn how to cope with unprecedented situations. Think of public speaking as a process. It starts with you. You are the initiator of a speech, presentation, or event, and you have the knowledge, credibility, and preparation under the belt, to share a topic with an audience. It's a great privilege, and you should take pride in the fact that you are, in a sense, leading others with your words.

2. Message.

This element encompasses what you are going to say to those that are watching you. It is crucial to do proper research. You must consider the audience to whom you are speaking to and think about how what you say will make them feel. Today, especially, saying anything remotely controversial can blow things out of proportion. Because there are many subjects society is sensitive too, when approaching a political or social topic, be aware that it will most likely be judged by someone, if not most people you are delivering the speech to. Consider and reconsider what you are saying, but at the same time, speak from the heart. Don't be afraid of being judged by others for speaking your truth or mind, but do consider whether the points you make are worth it and properly conveyed for everybody to understand them equally. To be outspoken about sensitive topics, you have to accept the judgment and be willing to deal with it constructively.

3. Channel.

The channel is what makes communication between you and your audience possible. If you think about how public speeches were conducted previously, you would recall that there was not much to it because there was only one way of doing it, before the radio was made available that is. Today, public speaking isn't considered a formal-only event. It includes announcements, presentations, and yes, speeches by politicians, economists, activists, and many kinds of people from all walks of life. The channels used include public and social platforms, like a radio, phone, or even a video conference, with two of the most typically recognized as Zoom or Skype today. There are different mediums to work with today, which is helpful when you struggle with public speaking. Sometimes, speaking into a phone or broadcasting a speech without people in front of you can seem a lot less stressful, which is why people choose it to cope with the challenges associated with public speaking. Even if it doesn't allow you to work on real public speaking skills, it does help you practice how to speak in front of others, which can help you have a better experience with public speaking in front of a physical audience when the time comes.

4. Listener.

Consider who you are talking to. Without your audience, you may as well be talking to a wall, which is why you should prioritize them. Even if you only have a few people listening to your message, you can still provide them value and learn from speaking in front of different sizes of crowds. It may sound strange but sometimes, speaking in front of a lot of people feels better than speaking in front of two to ten people. Whereas, it's the other way around for others. Focus on what your listener needs to hear, wants to hear, and what they can learn from you. Considering these elements, you know you can bring value to them, which makes the point of placing yourself in a vulnerable position to speak or perform, much more bearable and worth it. If you have a purpose, the process almost becomes worth it. Keep in mind why you are doing what you are doing, only if you are not forced to do it, that is. Maintain a purpose.

5. Feedback.

    Dividing your speech into two parts, focus the first part on talking about the information and message itself, and the second part, a Q & A section that allows you to interact with your audience, and in doing so, get to know them. It will make you and your audience feel more comfortable and allow you to receive feedback and opinions from them. You can learn a lot from this section of your speech, and so can they. The point of it is for them to comprehend what you've said better, which simultaneously will aid your confidence, expand your knowledge about how your audience feels, think, and respond to what you are saying, and finally, give you clarity on how to improve.

6. Interference.

    There will always be things that get between what you have prepared and obtained the perfect outcome. Just as mentioned previously, perfectionism is non-existent in public speaking. No matter how much you prepare, anything can happen, and anybody can respond to what you say in their unique and opinionated manner. With this in mind, the best way to deal with unexpected things is to focus on the relationship between you and your listeners. If you can maintain a strong relationship and be honest with them, what happens around you won't matter. If you can block out negativity or interruptions, you will have a successful speaking session, regardless of what's happening around you. The best thing you can do in any situation is to keep your audience focused on the topic and not any elements or disturbances around you.

7. Situation.

    Taking this element into account, by picking the time and place of the event, you can troubleshoot potential issues and get comfortable with where you will be delivering your speech. You can even practice where you will speak, and within the time frame, you are given to get an idea of how your speech should go. You can set goals for each topic without putting any pressure on yourself or going too fast. Being comfortable with the location of your event will make you feel more confident on the day thereof.

Chapter 2: Verbal Communication

Communicating is essential for all life to function optimally. Everybody communicates in their way, even the animals, plants, and winds. Verbal communication is the sharing of information between two or more people. It is what we use to get our message across, to say what we want and sometimes need to say. Verbal communication doesn't only include communication through speaking, but it also includes writing. It can be whatever way you choose to deliver or exchange information, which means we use it in our everyday lives. It is especially relevant in public speaking. First, you write what you want to say, and then you deliver it verbally to a few people or a big audience. Of course, verbal communication is not just talking, it's about the words you choose, how they come across, and the manner they are interpreted. If you don't speak clearly, those who listen to you can misinterpret you, or if you are addressing a specific audience, but other people in your audience won't necessarily get the same takeaway from your speech, it could be ineffective. Sometimes, it could also be offensive, which is something that today, you are advised to avoid.

Verbal communication is often mistaken for just including speaking words, but writing it is just as significant. With public speaking, you cannot speak unless you prepare. Writing down what you want to say helps because seeing it in front of you, you will get to dissect everything to ensure the interpretation of your message is clear and thoroughly understood. Doing this repeatedly can teach you a lot about how to speak to the receivers of the message you are trying to convey.

Taking this into account, you can understand why it is required to understand verbal communication and treat it like a skill to reflect on and clarify the message you are trying to share with the world. If you are uncertain about the things you say, people will have a difficult time believing you. One of the most helpful keys to public speaking is to always be true to who you are. If you are fake and pretentious, you will fail to come across as believable, and those who listen to you won't respect you or give you the time of day to hear what you have to say.

For effective verbal communication, there are a few elements you need to work on, including things like body language, facial expressions, and the tone of your voice. These are, of course, just a few things, but imagine only one of them was out of place. You wouldn't be able to convince your audience to listen to you or keep them interested in what you are saying. That is also why it is crucial to get a hold on your nervousness. Some people experience it badly, while others feel a little uneasy before they have to do a speech. Nervousness is something difficult to tackle. To most people, it seems impossible to control, but it will show if it's there, and that's why you have to practice as much as you can–not your speech, but communicating effectively with other people. If you are comfortable speaking to one person at a time, consider speaking to two people, and increasing that number until you start to feel comfortable with it. Be sure to get used to interpersonal encounters first before you amend the numbers.

Understanding what you are saying is equally necessary because only when you have clarity of speech can you remain focused, calm, and polite. If you are confident about what you want to say, the entire process of delivering a speech becomes easier. It will increase your confidence because when you deliver it, you will know what to say and with that, understand your audience. You will realize that there is nothing to be afraid of, and even if you make mistakes, you'll know how to recover from them. Your audience will, in return, respect you for it. It is a comforting thought to people who have already nailed public speaking.

When you start, it may seem like you are never going to complete it. It may seem like forever, especially on a big podium in front of dozens or hundreds of people. When you are opening your speech, keep in mind that it is the first impression many people will get of you, so make it good. It adds a lot of pressure to the table, but if you can get past the first few minutes of your speech and win over your audience, you will do well. It's always helpful to tell the people you are talking to more about who you are. You don't have to elaborate, but giving them an insight into who they are listening to will give the speech an element of personal, and if you can become relatable, you will be set for success. If you can manage to make a good first impression, people will always come back to hear more of what you have to say. Over time, this builds respect, until people will go out of their way to see you, or even pay to see you speak. Always remain conscious of your first impression. Remember that, although you have done speeches in the past, you may be standing in front of a new audience every time you do a speech. No pressure.

Before you dive into everything you have to master for proper verbal communication, consider the main areas of effective speaking:

1. Choose the words carefully.
2. Learn how to speak the words.
3. Combine verbal preparation with non-verbal communication.

This three-step guide can be a foundation for building your speech that you can build on. Since all of these elements affect the transmission of the message you are trying to get across, you must consider the words you choose and use different words, almost like you are writing a good essay. You don't want to be repetitive or redundant with what you are saying. If you feel like you are repeating yourself, consider it an indication that you need to either revise your speech or do more research and add more information, keeping in mind that it remains relevant to the message you want to deliver. If keeping it shorter is better to preserve the quality of the information, keep the speech section brief, and add a bigger Q & A section to the speech. Of course, if you do this, ensure you are ready for it and well versed in how you will answer the questions. For some people, the Q & A part of a speech is easier to do, while for others, not knowing what is going to be asked is nerve-wracking. Either way, be ready.

Learning how to speak words is as important as the words you choose. Again, if you don't know what it is you're talking about, it will be noticed, and people will become disinterested in what you are saying. You don't want to bore the audience, so turn the information you share into a knowledgeable experience for everyone. Don't just share what you know. It's like printing out the Encyclopedia and reading while occasionally glancing at the audience to check whether everybody is still there. No. Be creative with the way you speak and portray a message. Keeping your audience engaged is how you will deliver a good speech.

With the purpose of your speech, you can write a sufficient and value-worthy piece to deliver to your audience. Once you have done this, you can move on to the delivery thereof. Analyzing your audience helps you know how to deliver your speech. Although the elements need to be practiced and perfected in a comfortable way that will keep your audience engaged, you must keep in mind who you are speaking to.

Pitch

The pitch of your voice is one of many elements that need to be in sync with what you speak. It adds to the manner of how you portray what you want to say and allows for gaining control over your voice. Pitch is necessary to understand your voice at all times, including the tone thereof. If you don't know how to control pitch, then you won't be able to vary the tone of your voice, which will result in a one-toned boring speech and disengage the audience. That is not something you want. There is nothing worse than starting a speech, and when you are a few minutes in, you realize that you not only sound boring but that you are disconnected to your audience because of the way you speak. When you are in the moment, it can feel like that is it, your speech is ruined. You may also feel like you have lost the respect of those who are listening to you, which is why you need to work on your pitch.

Pitch can best be described as the highness and lowness of your voice. That is why a poor pitch can make you seem uninterested or like you lack passion for what you are saying to those who are watching you. In American English particularly pitch is crucial, especially in politics, social and cultural situations today. If you can learn how to control your pitch, you will know how to express different emotions and stress. What you sound like to others may not seem necessary to control when you speak, because let's be real. You speak to people every day. In a relaxed setting, it's probably not as important, but formally, it's of utmost importance. You do not want to deliver a message in the wrong way. Addressing pitch will make you sound more natural, less stressed, and more expressive. To do so, you have to consider the length, volume, and tone of your voice.

If you are native in a language, you will have a much better time to control or learn how to control pitch. However, non-native speakers that want to speak English proficiently, require a lot of practice. It's much more difficult to speak a language other than your native language impactfully as the tone may come across as flat. Since non-native speakers have not learned from a young age how to express themselves in English, they may sound monotone and robotic. Speaking unclearly can influence others' perceptions of you. In English, pitch variations are used in every sentence, and if it's not, you may be misunderstood. Given its importance, if you are preparing for a speech, you must start practicing your pitch. This doesn't require a vocal coach, but you can get help from one if you are non-native and feel like it's the best route for you.

Otherwise, think of improving your pitch as editing the way you speak with expressions to portray what you want to say. This can be done effectively by creating a pitch variation by going deeper into intonation, word stress, and reducing your accent. By practicing your speech, you can recognize parts that you can emphasize, particularly the things you want to highlight, the concept, and the goal of the speech.

Consider this exercise to practice your pitch effectively:

First start by focusing on the baseline pitch, which is what you use when you rest your voice. Think of a basic sound like 'da' or 'ma' and repeat it using the lowest pitch you have. Then, increase your pitch by repeating the sound a single step above your baseline pitch. Then, after practicing this for a while, continue increasing it gradually, almost like you are walking stairs. Notice the possibilities in your voice and that you don't only have one tone, but many. With this in mind, scale it back to either one or two steps above your baseline. See how easy it is to switch from one pitch to another?

Keeping your pitch steady, go a step below your baseline pitch, and familiarize yourself with the different possibilities in the pitch of your voice. It should be natural. Don't force a pitch that you do not have. You can continue this exercise by switching between more pitches and practice talking in them. Once you are comfortable with the switches, you can practice your speech using what you think is most effective. You can use it to produce word stress. It will help you place emphasis where necessary in your speech.

Practicing pitch does not have to be a big thing. You should make time to improve yourself and the things you feel you lack or can do better in. You can become a natural by practicing just 3 to 5 minutes a day. It stretches your pitch, so think of it as making your voice more flexible.

Once you can control your pitch with effective word stress, you can improve the natural sound of your voice. The point of practicing the flexibility of your voice is to get so used to it becomes second nature, which means you won't have to focus on it when you are delivering your speech or any other conversation you find yourself in. When you look at different words and say them out loud, you will notice that there is a part in most words that carries emphasis, like the word 'presentation,' 'entertainment,' or 'teaching.'

Presen**ta**tion

Enter**tain**ment

Tea**ching**

There is an emphasis on most words. Apart from the sentence construction, by perfecting word stress, you can learn how to speak words and learn how to emphasize them when it is necessary or where it increases the effectiveness thereof. Pitch goes hand in hand with intonation to safeguard the tone of your voice, allowing you to make your speech more expressive.

Intonation

As a part of public speaking, intonation refers to both the tone modulation and pitch of your voice to add stress to relevant words. It is helpful to make a speech aid in the expressiveness of a speech. With it, you can transfer the emotion that you are providing a subject with, to show in the delivery of your words. It is relevant in instances of surprise, frustration, astonishment, or excitement in one's voice. When these emotions are expressed effectively, your audience will notice that you are passionate about what you are saying, which will make you more believable and genuine. People are generally also more attracted to passionate people and would rather listen to them than anyone that doesn't care about what they talk about.

Combining tone and pitch, intonation allows you to communicate various meanings as required to make your speech interesting. It can help you create a sense of curiosity, speculation, and excitement, which allows the audience to formulate their theories and conclusions, perhaps even a question that they will keep in mind even after your speech. It is impactful and can be communicated in four different types of pitches.

The four types of pitches include:

1. Rising intonation for increasing the voice's pitch gradually over time.
2. Falling intonation for when the pitch falls with time.
3. Dipping intonation which falls and then rises.
4. Peaking intonation which rises and then falls.

These different types of pitches are used consciously or unconsciously to convey various meanings to listeners.

As an example, it can be

- Informational: "**I saw a** man in the road" answers the questions, "What happened" or "Who did you see." But, when you say, "**I** saw a man on the road," it can answer the question, "Did you hear a man on the road." (3)
- Grammatical: A rising pitch can turn a statement into a question with either the answer yes or no. For instance, "**He's going** home." (4)
- Illocution: The intentional meaning gets highlighted by a pitch pattern. "**Why** don't you move to New York?" (Question - 3) versus "**Why don't you** move to New York?" (Suggestion - 4)
- Attitudinal: A high declining pitch indicated more excitement than a low-declining pitch. "**Good morn**ing" (high to low - 4 and 3) versus "**Good morn**ing." (continuous low - 3)
- Textual: Not found in sentences. It signals the absence of a statement ending in a pitch decline, "The conference was can**celed**." Here there is a high pitch on both of the syllables 'celed.' (3)

With public speaking, you can make changes to your pitch as you please and think is best. The pitch of your speech can be changed using a variety thereof. By practicing, you will be able to vary between the pitches naturally over time. When you prepare for your speech, avoid monotony, which is to speak with a single pitch tone that doesn't have any variety. Change up the pitches of your speech to add and remove emphasis where necessary. You can also practice your sentences with the help of intonation patterns for changing up the meaning thereof. Integrating pauses where adequate and effective can help you create a more structured speech, instead of just rambling it without stopping. In this way, you can allow your audience space to think about what you say during your pauses, and captivate them when you start speaking again. When you add pauses to your speech, be sure to add them at the right moments. It should enable you to collect your thoughts before presenting the climax of the speech, pause before utterance, help people gain clarity about what you want to communicate and deliver your appeal with renewed strength. Your pauses can prepare the listener to receive your message and are often advised to integrate into the preparation of a speech. It also creates effectiveness suspense, which sparks interest. When you are integrating pauses into your speech, you must avoid ineffective pauses, like speech disfluencies, filler words, and filled pauses.

The best way to work on your intonation is to record a conversation between you and another person. It can help you see how many pauses you use, including the relevancy thereof. Taking note of where you need to adjust yourself with practice is the best way to articulate your speech. When you record yourself, you will also be able to review the things you struggle with the most, like pronunciation or whether or not you are unclear. Once you know what it is your speech lacks, you can address it immediately.

Take note of articulation, which is the change of sounds from how you move your mouth that affects your vocal folds, like moving your tongue, teeth, and lips, all of which need to be controlled for effective speaking. After practicing, you will notice the sounds you struggle to pronounce, which can be addressed with the help of a speech therapist. If you are serious about public speaking or it forms a significant part of your occupation, this is something to consider wisely. Seeing a speech therapist doesn't mean that there is something wrong with the way you speak, it just means that you need to practice your skill of how you talk by addressing whatever it is you struggle with or lack. With practice, anything can be improved. By changing your pronunciation, you can change the way you speak words under stress, which can help you overcome sounding nervous in stressful situations.

Volume

As you learn more about public speaking, you start to understand what it takes to be successful in the process of speech delivery, and with that, the importance of effective vocal delivery. Since pitch is so essential in effective delivery, you can understand why it is required to focus on the volume of your voice, which is indicated by how soft or loud your voice is. It cannot be emphasized how necessary it is to pay attention to the volume of your voice. Of course, it will depend based on the setting you are in. Keep in mind the distance between you and your audience. Consider the setting, whether you will be speaking with or without a microphone, the range of your microphone. If you think about it clearly, you will have to adjust the volume of your speech if you are delivering it in a hall with a microphone versus on a field without a microphone.

If you don't have any amplification, you also have to keep in mind the distance of which your voice spans. If you naturally have a soft voice, you may want to consider a microphone. When you are not speaking in front of people, but a videoconference instead, you will have to ensure that your equipment is set to support your voice, whether it be naturally loud or have limitations. When you have a soft voice, it can seem very limiting to improve the delivery of your speech, which is why it is necessary to practice improving the volume of your voice. Regardless of what people think, you can work on the volume of your voice by practicing speaking in a big room. You can ask someone to accompany you and walk further and further away from you in the large room to see whether they can hear you properly. By knowing how loud you should speak, for the person at the back of the room to hear you, you will know how loud to speak. It can also aid in your pitch. You must also ensure you have space to move and breathe. When you are cramped, you may feel like you can't express yourself properly, or to the capacity of your volume abilities. Make sure you have enough space to deliver your speech. You can also practice speaking directly to people in different parts of the place you are speaking in.

When you use a microphone, you also have to consider the distance your voice travels, but also the range of the microphone. When you watch television, and the volume is too loud, it's unsettling. To put it simply, you can't enjoy it properly. The same goes for when the TV's volume is too low. The same goes for a microphone. If it is set too loud or too soft, your audience won't have a good experience listening to you speak, and then the work you have implemented to improve the verbal delivery of your voice won't matter.

There are different microphones you can use to support your speech and make you more comfortable. These include:

- Hand-held microphones - High-quality mics that allow you to isolate your diaphragm from any potential vibrations with suspension and foam padding. The difference between low quality and high-quality microphone is the presence of vibrations. The clearer your voice sound over a microphone, the more you can rest assured that you are using a quality mic.
- Stationary mics - This type of microphone is attached to podiums. Stationary mics can be limiting because you have to stand in one place throughout your entire speech. If you are delivering a formal speech, stationary mics are best. These are preferred with the delivery of very formal speeches. Of course, you have to take into account the length of the mic's connecting cable.
- Lavalier mics - These microphones are considered the most effective. They are very flexible and can be used in any setting. Using these, you can hide the cord thereof under your clothing and walk around freely while delivering your speech, without having to worry about a limitation on stage. They are some of the most modern and preferred types of microphones.

When you use a microphone of any kind, consider the following:

- Hold it six to eight inches away from your mouth and speak over it. Don't hold it too far from your mouth as the volume thereof will become significantly lower. You should also not hold it too close to your mouth as it will pick up your breathing.
- Choose the right microphone for you to ensure proper quality when you speak into it. Don't just opt for the first microphone available to you.
- Consider traditional mics over lavalier mics because lavalier mics aren't protected from handling noise. When you move too much or get bumped, it may throw off the sound quality of the mic. Keep this in mind when you are preparing to deliver a speech.
- Run a sound check with your microphone by testing the speakers in the room. It's recommended to practice delivering your speech before the day of the event so that you can make adjustments where it is necessary.

With the volume of your voice, also consider the rate that you are speaking per minute. You can time yourself to establish the rate that you speak at. A normal rate is 125 words a minute on average, which is what you should strive towards more or less. If you are speaking too many words per minute, you are rushing through your speech. The same goes for speaking too few words, which indicates you are dragging through it. It must be considered if you want to convey your message to your audience. Speaking too slow or too fast can either seem like you are uninterested in what you are talking about, or that you want to get it over with as fast as you can. Either way, you are showing that you don't care–something that must be avoided if you want to deliver an impactful speech.

When you are speaking, the best thing to do is change up the rate you speak at to ensure the audience knows the point of your message. In this sense, you don't have to be indicatively verbal about the things you want to focus on instead you can highlight it with the use and alignment of proper speech elements. When you speak, you should avoid maintaining one mood. It's not interesting and could place you at risk as being perceived to be boring. If you take it slower, not too slow, then you will also be able to think more clearly about what you want to say, which could prevent you from repeating yourself or holding back during times when energy is needed to fuel the speech. It is helpful to record yourself to check in with the pace you are speaking at.

Energy

If you want to become a meaningful and memorable speaker, you have to understand why it is necessary to have energy when you speak. That's because public speaking itself is a direct exchange of energy from you to the audience you speak to. By speaking with sufficient energy, you won't have anything to worry about, and you can rest assured that your audiences will return the same level of engagement or interest that you have shown in the way you speak. Without passion, a speech is merely words on a paper. If it is passionless or emotionless, even worse, meaningless, it will be recognized immediately. You will then come across as fake or uninteresting, and nobody wants to watch that. Not for long anyway.

You are better than sounding uninteresting. You can speak to your audience, captivate them, and come back later and do the same, but first, you have to learn how to be energized on stage. Just like nobody wants to listen to someone that isn't passionate about what he or she speaks about, nobody wants to listen to anyone that is one-toned and sounds as though they lack enthusiasm.

If you are not energized during your speech, you should keep in mind that even without being energized, you still give off energy, and it affects your audience. So, if you are negative, or in a bad headspace starting your speech, there is a good chance that your audience will also recognize your stage presence and pick up whatever it is you carry with you. That's because you are on display, especially on a stage or platform. It's not only your words people pay attention to, but also the way you speak, body language, and the way you look physically. If you look tired or too stressed, for instance, the chances are that nobody is going to take you as seriously as you want them to.

When you are energized, however, people feel it. Not only do you connect better with your audience, but your energy rubs off on them, which makes them feel good and excited to learn more about what you have to say. Now, some people hate public speaking, but for those who don't or are passionate about delivering a meaningful message, it is incredibly rewarding. Impacting people is probably one of the most challenging things you can do successfully, especially if you can also maintain it. You can learn a lot from public-influential speakers like Gary Vaynerchuk or Simon Sinek, both of which are inspirational and good-feeling speakers. When you watch them deliver a speech, whether it's a self-help speech or more about technology and trends, these speakers have one thing in common. They have earned the respect of their audiences by capturing their attention. It has been done as a result of the meaning and value they bring to the stage. If you want to master public speaking, these are good examples of people who have managed to master public speaking. Their energy is so powerful that they can capture the attention of audiences from the minute they step onto a stage, which is what you should strive to.

With a lot of practice and some help from referring to other influential speakers, there are many ways to show your audience that you are present and have the energy to speak with confidence and bring value.

It can be done by:

1. Be confident and passionate.

    When a speaker is confident, it's a given that their audience is more likely to trust them and what they say. If you are not confident and display signs of being uncertain about yourself or what you are saying, you won't win over the trust of your audience. People don't want to listen to others who think they know what they are talking about. They want to listen to those who are so sure about themselves and what they believe in that they can go in-depth about it. If you don't thoroughly understand what you are talking about, you can't advise anyone else on it, not to mention convincing them of what you are saying. Speaking to others is like putting your truth on display. If you are not confident about it, you are unlikely to be passionate about it, and people will be less likely to listen to you. You should also avoid playing it safe. When you choose a topic to talk about, make sure there's meaning to it. If it's something too basic or easy to talk about, you should adjust it to keep it interesting. The deeper you can go into a topic, the better.

2. Create a powerful opening and closing segment.

    The body of your speech is quite important but think about it. If you can't get your audience's attention at the beginning of your speech, you can forget about the rest of it. That's because, with the opening of your speech, your audience has already made up their mind about you. They have already considered whether what you are saying will be interesting enough and worth listening to. That's why you should mainly focus on the opening and closing of your speech. The opening is the main thing that will ensure a connection for the rest of your speech, while the closing will be the takeaway of the speech. It should make people think about what you've spoken about, and almost leave a thought for them to ponder on thereafter.

3. Indicate a relationship and journey.

    Having an audience or even a few people take time out of their day to listen to what you have to say is a blessing. It's more powerful and rewarding than most people think. Since you have the opportunity to make a difference or be impactful in any way, it's necessary to let your audience know that you want to go on a journey with them, and not just speak to get it over with. Public speaking is a long-term commitment. So, establishing an audience is important. The same goes for turning it into a sustainable one for your career. You should let your audience know where you will be going together and indicate a journey where they can learn more along the way. It's also helpful to have experience in public speaking, as it builds credibility over the years. Don't worry if you haven't had much experience or built up an audience yet, it's never too late to start, practice, and work your way to the top.

4. Become conversational.

   When you deliver a speech, you don't want to sound like a robot. You are, after all, human. And, you are speaking to other humans, and so, delivering a speech should be like having a conversation. Of course, there must be some structure and formality to your speech, but think about it, if you treat it like a conversation, you will be far less stressed, and it will be much easier to deliver a good speech. It's always a good feeling to have in knowing that you are doing well. It boosts your confidence and makes you feel like you can be a successful public speaker. Many people have one or two bad experiences with public speaking and find it difficult to perform well thereafter due to a lack of confidence. Some people also take it way too seriously. Yes, delivering a speech is a big undertaking, but it's only a big deal if you make it out to be. It doesn't have to be constrictive. Any stress you have in your mind about it, again, is only as big as you make it out to be. If you treat your speech like having a conversation, it will feel more relaxed and much easier to do. You may even enjoy it, and when you do, it becomes incredibly rewarding.

5. Be clear and concise.

   Could you imagine if you weren't clear about the information you share with the people that are listening to you? It wouldn't be good, and like it or not, people will notice. When they do, more people will know about it, and you will become less credible, which is probably one of the worst things that could happen to a public speaker. Your reputation is quite important in the field of public speaking. If you have shared the wrong information with your audience, nobody would likely want to listen to you again. Depending on the extent thereof, it can also get you into a lot of trouble, so you have to be clear about the information you share. Apart from being clear on the information you share, you have to speak clearly and concisely. Since people are listening to what you are saying, and you are speaking throughout your speech, people can't exactly tell you to repeat yourself. So, you have to be clear on what you want to say and speak it clearly, while also being concise to show people you care about what you are saying.

6. Own the stage.

   When you are speaking publicly on a platform, the stage is yours, and you should own it. When you are standing on a big stage, it can feel a bit daunting because all the attention is diverted to you. The key is to use any platform you have the privilege of standing on to your advantage. Instead of thinking of it as something scary or considering how big it is, think that you have a platform to stand on and speak your wisdom and share your truth with the world. Having a voice that can make an impact is highly valued today, which should be appreciated. When you change your perspective about a big stage or the number of people you are speaking to, everything becomes easier and more purposeful. Since you are likely to be the only one standing on the stage, make it a space of comfort that you use as a tool to your advantage.

7. Work on storytelling skills.

    Storytelling is an element you can use to personalize a speech and make it more interesting. Sometimes, the information you have to share with others is very grey. There's not a lot of color to it, and if it is repetitive, it can seem a bit boring. Storytelling is something you can use to liven up your speech. It can also be used to emphasize specific topics or advice, especially if you are delivering a self-help speech. It can even carry your speech, almost creating a structure–something you can refer back to that will make it more relatable for the people who are watching you. Stories have a powerful effect on people's emotional responses, which can be used as another helpful tool to keep your audience intrigued and ponder on the thoughts you introduce to them. Today, storytelling is implemented by some of the best-ranked public speakers. Without it, speeches can seem very boring.

8. Notice your language and vocal dynamics.

    Your voice should be treated as an asset when you deliver a public speech. It's one of the most significant elements you use to deliver whatever it is you want to say or share with the world and should be treated accordingly. When you practice your speech, it's helpful to listen to how you speak. If your pitch is too low, you will seem uninteresting, and if it is too high, you may come across as irritating or like you are trying too hard. Either way, it won't get your message across successfully, and you definitely won't have won over the attention of your audience. That's why you need to keep the tone of your voice level, use proper English, or the language you are speaking in. Ensure you know who your audience is so that you know what to say and how to say it. Equally, you should know what not to say. Practice being aware of how you use words, how to say it to make them more effective during your speech, and where to adjust anything ineffective.

9. Use metaphors.

    Just like you use storytelling as a tool to make your speech more dynamic and interesting, more elements can be used to do so. One of those includes metaphors. It can make your speech more memorable as it can create a sense of excitement when you are speaking. Using comparisons creatively can make you and what you are saying more relatable without it seeming like you are trying too hard. Implementing it is a helpful way to grab your audience's attention immediately and can be used to spice up your speech.

10. Make the message meaningful.

Without energy, your message just consists of words that seem like they are supposed to mean something. Without a message, your energy won't have any purpose to deliver what could be great.

When you are writing your speech, keep this in mind. There is a reason why people come to watch you speak. If you are a good public speaker, they will want to hear what you have to say, and even tell others about you. That's the power of impact. Without being impactful, public speaking is ineffective. It doesn't even matter what you believe enough to prepare and talk about. As long as you believe what you are saying or want to say to the world, you are on the right track. Just like a teacher has to fulfill the role of someone who passes knowledge to others or makes them skilled in something, you have to embody your speech. Teachers believe in what they are teaching, and so should you. When you are a public speaker professionally, and you know what you want to say to the world, perhaps even strive to build a stigma around it, you too are a teacher. With that, you have power in your hands—the chance to change the way people think, highlight causes, and start movements to change them.

Pauses

There are moments in our days.

There are moments when we work.

There are moments when we speak.

So, speak with intent and bring your worth.

Everybody has something to offer the world. Some can be constructive in what they say, while others are more helpful in moments of silence. Similarly, there are moments that it is necessary to speak, and then moments that there are not. With public speaking, pausing may not seem significant at first, yet it is. It's that thing that has a bigger effect than you realize. The same goes for the effect of a pause in a conversation. If you think about it, a pause can have the power in making people think about what you are saying. Particularly, when a pause follows a question or an idea. It can be very effective.

Every good speaker is skilled at pausing, and so, it should be treated as a skill.

One of the things most people tend to fail at is using too many words. When you are given a certain period to deliver a speech, the last thing you should do is try and fill the minutes with as much information you can. Think of it as a sponge that can only be squeezed till a certain point for water to come out of it. Eventually, it won't contain any water. With a speech, you can only speak so much before it loses meaning, which is also why pauses help. It fills little spaces–moments–in your speech that can make the message you want to convey all the more effective. Even though the structure thereof consists of only words, gestures, movements, and the moments you pause are equally important. Without it, a speech can seem impaired or incomplete. If a speech lacks effectiveness, it can sound like you are speaking a never-ending sentence. When implementing pauses, you don't have to make them long. They can be short and sweet– just enough time to make people wonder about what you are going to say next.

Pausing during your speech is also helpful if you need to collect your thoughts. In this case, you can pause longer. It may seem inadequate at times, but with practice, you'll get used to implementing it. Before you know it, integrating pauses into your speech will be natural. They work best when they are integrated naturally. When you are writing or reciting your speech, you don't have to plan where to implement pauses. You can add them during your speech as you work through it. It shouldn't seem disruptive to your audience. It is something you should be cautious with. The best way to know what is appropriate and what's not is to get to know your audience. If you know your audience well enough, you'll know what's disruptive or adequate to them. Adding anything to your speech should only improve it, not take away from it.

There are many different ways you can use a pause. Primarily, it is used to enhance your speech and includes:

- The emphasis pauses.

    Using a pause to add emphasis to a sentence or speech as a whole is one of the most basic and common ones you practice with. Although it may seem like the speech you've written has enough emphasis, reading it aloud without any breaks in between can come across like you are rushing your speech. Not implementing pauses is very ineffective if you want to deliver a speech that portrays how passionate you are about what you are saying. Since passion plays an essential part in a speech, you can understand why pauses are required for effect. If you don't believe in adding pauses to a speech, record yourself delivering it without them. You will realize that it doesn't sound quite right and finally grasp why pauses are needed. Pauses that get added for emphasis can signal to say something significant, an idea or thought listeners should keep in mind. It can also indicate something that listeners must take away from your speech. Even if an extended pause can seem unnecessary, it's not. You can extend your pause until you feel it's the right moment to deliver your point.

- The punchline pause.

It's not always easy to add humor to a speech, not for everyone, anyway. That is because everybody is different. Some are naturally funnier than others, and that's just the way it is. However, just because you aren't naturally funny, doesn't mean you cannot work at it. It does not mean you can't practice making jokes or working humor into your speech. Besides, you should keep in mind that making a joke on stage takes longer to register with an audience. So, unless you won't be fazed by the jokes you make that may or may not receive a response, you make use of conversational humor. If you are daring with jokes, then implementing pauses at the right moments can help you get the response you want from your audience. You can take comedians as examples. Stand-up comedy includes many instances of punchline pauses that you may find useful when you are writing and practicing your speech.

- The dramatic pause.

Like a pause for emphasis, the dramatic is used to indicate something. Its purpose is to build up to create a build-up, which follows an intro. After the build-up, there is either a surprise twist or something big that happens. It increases tension before the twist or punchline. The pause must be long enough to be interesting, but not too long to make listeners disinterested in what you are saying. Consider using a dramatic pause for the length of one deep breath, which is more than enough. The pause creates a sense of basic excitement or to create dramatic tension. Think of the dramatic pause as something that is not serious. It can be considered as winking to your audience. It can be sarcastic, humoristic, or theatrical. Some may be careful with adding dramatic pauses to a speech, but with practice, they become natural. Since they are so effective in a speech, it's worth practicing and giving it a shot until it becomes easy to implement.

- The lead-in pause.

This type of pause is similar to the dramatic pause in the sense that it builds up to a point that follows with something significant that you want your listeners to take in and remember. It can also be a pivoting point in a speech or indicate the point of it. It indicates that you are taking them on a new path and that they should be alert the moment you commence. With this pause, tension is built up slowly and released in a more relaxed way as you move on to the next point. You can treat this pause as a little break or reposition yourself on stage. You can choose whether you want to be theatrical with this pause or not. If you are a beginner, you can ease into it, and keep the pause short to start.

- The break pause.

    It's not an easy task to be on stage, and your audience is well aware thereof. Well, most are. There can be instances where you have a difficult crowd of listeners. They may even be very judgmental, serious, or opinionated. You can imagine how stressful this must be. However, for the most part, the people who come to see you speak should be lenient and understanding that what you are doing isn't easy and that those who do it are brave. It is accompanied by respect, which makes the whole thing seem much better to carry out, and successfully too. The break pause is for you and your audience. It is implicit and serves as a moment that you can self-reflect in front of your audience. It is a very vulnerable pause, and if you are not comfortable with your audience, feel free to ease into it or reserve it for the next speech. But, it can be helpful because it creates a moment that you can ponder until you move on to your next point, especially if it's a big or important one. You should trust your audience to understand you because you comprehend them. Keep in mind that a speech doesn't only consist of high-points, but times of rest too.

Pauses are natural. They don't have to be planned, but if you feel better with the idea that there are breaks in your speech and that it balances it, then it's good to plan for it. Implementing pauses should not feel like a stressful thing that disrupts the flow of your speech. It should improve it. Since pauses can't be practiced, unless it's in front of an audience, think of points of your speech where they will be the most useful. When you speak in front of people, you will know exactly where to place them. If you are comfortable with your speech, you will surprise yourself with how well you can deliver a speech with pauses.

Pronunciation

Your speech is made up of words, and whether you are speaking in front of an audience or one on one with someone, the way words are said and sound is crucial for proper communication. Talking seems easy. Unless you have a problem with speech, it should be easy to speak, right?

It's not true. Stress forms a big part in the outcome of public speaking, or even speaking to one person for some. It's the one thing that keeps us from performing our best. It affects so many different things, but it especially affects pronunciation negatively. Pronunciation forms a part of verbal communication and can be perfected to make speech seem attractive and effective. It plays a significant role in the sound dynamics delivery of all languages. If you have a second language or are learning a new one, it's necessary to pay attention to pronunciation. People with strong accents in their native languages are prone to have a more difficult time shaking off bad pronunciation habits to speak adequately in a new language. It is a difficult thing to overcome, and can only be done with practice. Students who learn new languages are recommended to make time for conversing with other people in those languages, apart from learning the rules on how to speak different sounds.

Proper pronunciation requires the use of good rhythm, voice stress, and intonation of words in spoken language. Even if English is your first language, you are still likely to speak it differently than the next person. That's because it is spoken in various ways. However, as long as it sounds clear, there's not much to be worried about. If people have a difficult time understanding you, that's when you should address it. Of course, pronunciation has a lot to do with the location of where you grew up, your current location, possible speech impairments, ethnicity, education, and socio-economic class. Pronunciation focuses on an individual sound, just like articulation does. It can also focus on a sequence of sounds used in a single word, such as clever: cle + ver.

Syllable sounds are phonological building blocks of words, where single-syllable words, like the word 'cat,' is referred to as a monosyllable. Similar terms include disyllable, which indicates a word that consists of two syllables. There is also a trisyllable that consists of a word with three syllables or words with more than one syllable. With pronunciation, the main objective is to recognize various syllables that make up words. When you can recognize it, only then will you know where to apply stress to the correct syllable or how to use the correct pitch pattern for intonation–the tool that adds function to words to differentiate between different types of questions, statements, requests, and commands.

With public speaking, pronunciation must be on point. After all, people are listening to what you have to say, and if you are not clear, they won't understand you. It will make your speech pointless as the main objective of it is to tell people something they can think about or learn from. The point is to inform others about your beliefs, specialties, ideas, truths, or whatever it is you are speaking about, which is why it should be delivered correctly.

There are mechanics associated with pronunciation, as with the formation of different words. The lips, tongue, and other movable parts of the mouth, all work together for us to talk. With speech, the first thing you have to do is breathe properly. When you breathe, air enters your storage chamber, and then phonation takes place–a process that forces air into vibration with the action of your vocal folds. Then resonation takes place. It occurs when your mouth, throat cavities, and nose amplify audible sound. Finally, articulation occurs–a modification of sound that occurs as a result of the movement of your tongue, teeth, and lips, which creates recognizable patterns that you revert to when you have to use it again. Eventually, the more you use it, it becomes second nature to implement. In the English language, there are merely forty-four sounds that you have to master, which is supposed to be learned during childhood with the imitation of sounds that you hear. By becoming effective in making simple sounds, you can articulate it into repetitive sounds, and then combinations and words.

Since your audience needs to comprehend what you are saying, you have to make sure that you master these sounds to become an effective speaker. If you are struggling to make sounds properly during adulthood, consulting a speech therapist can be helpful.

To speak well, you shouldn't substitute or omit sounds with words. It's helpful to also steer clear of adding alternative sounds to worlds when you speak. Equally, you should pay attention to simple sound substitutions, which can include 't' for 'th' in a word, if you say 'tin' instead of 'thin.' You can also practice reading and record sections or chapters that include sounds that may appear problematic for you to pronounce. Once again, you listen to yourself, then listen to the correct word, which can be typed in on Google search and listened to, and adjust it where necessary.

Dialect

Along with pronunciation, dialect must be understood and implemented appropriately to deliver what is considered a good speech. Dialect refers to a variety of either one or several languages. It is a specific characteristic of a group that speaks a language and is distinguished by grammar, vocabulary, and pronunciation. It is often applied to patterns of regional speech and is used accordingly, depending on your audience. Dialect is divided into three primary categories, which include North American, British, and Australasian.

American English dialect is used mainly in the United States. Although there are many other languages and dialects thereof, this type of English is most commonly used by the federal government. Thus, it is considered a de facto language of the U.S. due to its widespread use throughout the country. When children go to school, this is the primary dialect they will be taught in, and general society converse in most states. The American English dialect has official status by only 28 out of 50 states. Hence, when you travel to different places in the U.S., you will notice different dialects. Some of the most common being New England, Inland North American, Mid-Atlantic, North Central, Midland American, Southern English, and Western English.

The mentioned dialects are all spoken in the U.S., and as a result, people can possess more than one dialect, which is wonderful as it allows for vocal variety. However, it can become confusing at times, especially when it comes to what is considered the correct American English dialect by the world. One dialect is not better than another in the U.S., yet North American is preferred. Whichever dialect is spoken by someone in power, that is usually the dialect accepted as a whole in a state. Sometimes, people who have only one dialect view others with more than one as having cultured backgrounds. Even though this is a good thing and not a bad thing, it is often portrayed negatively, particularly when it gets spoken in states that are strict about or proud of the way they speak. It is significant to consider, depending on where you deliver a speech. If you are uneducated about various dialects in different states, you should do proper research to avoid potentially offending people in certain states.

Again, having multiple dialects is a good thing due to having a bigger vocal variety. However, keep in mind that you should consider whether most of the members in your audience share the same one as you. With that, you must also ensure that the pronunciation of words is met in the appropriate dialect when speaking to audience members with a different one. When you speak to a national audience, you must choose your words carefully and wisely, and always pay attention to your pronunciation. If you speak multiple dialects, it is necessary to speak in your home dialect, which is preferably adopted by the majority of people to whom you speak to.

When you speak in front of people, whether it is a few or many, you will notice that with multiple dialects, you will have a greater variety of words to choose from, which is honestly an advantage to you. Some methods can be implemented to help create better variety in your word delivery, which includes speaking faster and slower and varying between the two with ease, and speaking with different pitches ranging from low to high and vice versa. It can also include increasing your force to speak softer or louder and pausing at specific points with ease during your speech to create a more natural effect.

Creating emphasis with any of these methods allows you to speak words and sentences faster. It creates improved consistency and word flow. It can be very beneficial for capturing the attention of your audience, especially when you want to create an effect at specific points in your speech. Emphasis will allow you to not only compare but also contrast. It will help you use different elements to speak at your most efficient pace, pitch, tone, and create pauses where it is necessary.

When speaking in a particular dialect, note that every speech contains key points that you can emphasize. These points must be identified to create the perfect delivery. You never want your speech to be flat and too simple. You want it to have a variety to be interesting. If you can identify the points where you can place emphasis, you can change the delivery thereof for it to either stand out or create contrast at the most effective points. Changing the rate of which you speak frequently is helpful, but you should always be aware that you should not talk at a rate that is too fast to get your speech done faster. It is not the point and won't help you whatsoever. Changing the rate of your speech should be natural, like with a conversation. By noticing how people change the rate at which they speak during a conversation, you can adopt tips from it and do the same. Once you understand why people speak at various rates and how effective it sounds, you can practice doing the same while delivering your speech.

Articulation

When you recite a speech, you are preparing to speak it the best you can. That is the point of reciting a speech. However, there is always a risk of overdoing it. And, while it can appear harmless to your speech, the last thing you want to be is too well-rehearsed. Because, although you have your speech locked in, knowing it too well is not too interesting for those who listen to you.

We get it, the 21st century is all about building robots and making them as effective as possible, but you are not a robot. If your audience wanted to listen to someone speak like a robot, they would Google the topic you are talking about and go listen to a system read whatever they've been programmed to say.

Since you are human, you need to feel what you say and show it. Otherwise, there is a good chance that your audience won't appreciate what you are saying to them.

Articulation in public speaking refers to how well we speak. It is a measure of our perceived education or intellect and is judged based on how good we are at articulating things. It includes how well we speak, whether we speak correctly, how we form vowels and consonants, and use our tongue, jaw, lips, and palate to formulate sounds identified as speech. Articulation plays a significant role in the delivery of our vocals, and even though we speak a lot during the day, when we are required to speak formally, we need to pay more attention to detail in preparing for formal speech presentations.

Just like pitch, tone, pronunciation, and dialect, articulation can be developed by any speaker, which means that everybody that has been given the time to learn and dedicate themselves can become profound public speakers.

To become more articulate in how you speak, you can:

- Listen to yourself.

    When you have conversations with others or, by any chance have a recording of yourself speaking, listen to yourself speak. Don't just speak. Take in what you are saying and how you are saying it. Is it the most effective way you can speak? Whether you talk to a coworker or friend, or in front of many people, you should be able to maintain a natural conversation. Identifying habits that make you sound either awkward or uncomfortable will be beneficial for you because once you identify them, you can address it and improve yourself.

- Evaluate the speed you talk at.

    Some people talk fast and sound interesting while others talk slowly and sound more concise about what they say. Other times, talking too fast can seem uneasy and disruptive, while talking too slow can come across as boring and inefficient. With practice, evaluate the rate at which you speak. You can speak slowly or faster where it is appropriate, but be sure that you don't go overboard with it. It helps to speak in front of someone or multiple people before you deliver your speech, as other people can give their opinions for you on how to improve before you deliver it to a big audience.

- Eliminate unnecessary words.

    To be more articulate is helpful when it comes to delivering the best version of yourself, or in this case, your speech, that you possibly can. Being more articulate is something to strive towards. No matter what your relationship with speech delivery is, whether you are comfortable or uncomfortable with it, there is always room for improvement. When you catch yourself saying the words 'um,' 'uh,' or 'like' frequently, it sounds like you are second-guessing yourself, which suggests that you are uncertain about what you are saying or want to say. That's the opposite of being articulate. Being accurate and sure about what you say is crucial for the proper delivery of a speech. If it doesn't bother you when you get stuck at times, it will greatly affect the way your audience views you and alter their opinion about whether you are worth listening to. Even if saying the words, 'um' or 'like' is merely a habit, it's not going to help you win over an audience. The best thing you can do with such words, commonly recognized as filler words, is to be conscious about saying them. By recognizing what you are saying to them, you can stop yourself in your tracks and replace them with better, more eloquent transitions. Consider taking the word "um" and replacing it with the phrase, "let's look at/ move on to…" It is a natural transition that can give you space to either recollect your thoughts quickly or mention another handy thought, idea, or piece of information. In this way, you can cover up your filler word without making it obvious.

- Focus on the sound you want to achieve.

With every word you speak, it's necessary to consider what you sound like. When you speak to people that have the same dialect and accent as you, it's easier to communicate and understand each other, even with the presence of slang or lazy English. However, when you speak to someone that has a different dialect or accent, you have to handle it differently. You can't mumble. In this case, you have to make an effort to pronounce every syllable precisely. It can be done by paying attention to the last words you use in sentences, which are usually altered depending on how you are used to speaking. When you speak with various types of people, you need to be clear and concise, especially when you are delivering a speech where the comprehension thereof should be on par.

- Study how other people speak.

You don't have to buy a ticket to an event where somebody professional is going to speak to watch public speakers. You can type in the name of a speaker that inspires you in a search engine or YouTube, and voila, watch endless hours of their public speeches. If you don't want to watch how someone speaks publicly, you can also look for a podcast and evaluate how different people speak. When a person speaks publicly regularly or has attention on them permanently, they are likely to be well versed in what they want to say. They have made a point of working out any kinks they may have had in their speeches, which is why listening to them is helpful. You can then identify your mistakes and address them accordingly.

- Exude confidence.

Being inarticulate is the complete opposite of confidence. The more confidence you have with speaking, the more precise you will be. Being confident requires you to get your anxiety and stress under control. It indicates that you know how to deal with it. Without anxieties and stressors, all that's left is your speech. If you can think this way and make it happen, there is a big chance that you will thrive in the delivery of you. Besides, confidence has a way of winning over the crowd. It can be displayed in many ways and is always respected by those who are watching you. If you are generally a very nervous speaker, you can try little tricks to make yourself seem more confident. It can be done by walking and sitting up straight, dressing for success but ensuring you are comfortable in your clothes at all times, and paying attention to body language, like not moving your hands or fidgeting too much.

- Address weaknesses.

  People who can't admit that they have weaknesses can never evolve past what they know. In public speaking, it is almost a duty to improve yourself as much as you can, and consistently too. Once you've identified all your weaknesses, you can create a solid plan to tackle them. You can write them all down, big and small, and address them equally one per day or week. However, if you decide to spend one week on a weakness you best practice a solution for it daily and not get out of the habit of being aware of them or think that you deserve a break to improve yourself. Eliminating filler words or learning how to form words with proper articulation are both examples of weaknesses you can address. You can repeat this process week after week until speaking fluently, concisely, clearly, and without any other element constraint, becomes easy and automatic for you.

Chapter 3: Non-Verbal Communication

Public speaking is known for creating a lot of negative feelings. For every ten people, you can bet more than a couple dollars on it that 50% or more of those individuals either have trouble or anxiety with public speaking. You can be sure that most people don't like it either because of its unpredictability.

People like being sure about what's going to happen next. Most people need to know what lies ahead in the future. It makes them feel like they have a handle of things and are in control. In anything or case where this lacks, people are prone to succumb to stress, excessive worry, and even depression at times. Being sure about what's going to happen next all the time is no way to live. It's very limiting, and while some individuals are happy and content with living planned and structured lives, according to schedule to ensure they know what they are doing or going to do at all times, it's no way to LIVE.

In terms of delivering a public speech, the thing standing between people that want to do it and those that are unwilling to do it off the bat is the relationship they have with unpredictability. The people who are not comfortable with it will go out of their way to avoid it at all costs.

You know which one you are. Perhaps you are in between, and you don't know how to quite make up your mind about whether you are at ease with delivering a speech in front of a lot of people or not. It may be dread, fear, nervousness, or excitement that you experience, but one thing is certain. The relationship you have with public speaking has everything to do with how you think about it. If you don't like it, it's probably because you are fearful of it or an element associated with it. It can be displayed through non-verbal communication, and especially through verbal communication. Think of non-verbal communication as something that safeguards the verbal side of it. With verbal communication, there's hardly any filter. Sure, you can cover your mistakes or become better versed in the words you speak, perhaps even speak the appropriate dialect as tailored for your audience, but that's it. Non-verbal communication doesn't involve speaking with words, which is why you can use it to support verbal communication or to show that you indeed have confidence and certainty about what you say.

Non-verbal communication includes means of communication that are not written or spoken language. Instead, it's the things we do that make our speech more believable. It can make us appear more inviting, comfortable, and sure of ourselves, which is very attractive to the eyes of audience members. If you can perfect your non-verbal communication skills, verbal communication can become easier. If you consider how you feel when someone is on stage speaking or performing, and they seem uneasy, stressed, or show symptoms of complete nervousness, you aren't exactly comfortable watching them. You may even feel sorry for them and want them to stop. So, really, when you think about it, it all becomes clear. You need to initiate and maintain a good relationship with your audience. You need to be comfortable so that they can be comfortable, which can be done with the proper body language, eye contact, moment, and appearance. These things are much easier to address than verbal communication elements at times, so working on them, as you do on your verbal communicative elements, is a constructive way to master what you want to achieve on stage.

Think of verbal communication as hearing what isn't said. The way you carry yourself—especially in silence. That's a good example. The dash (–) communicates to your audience without words, sometimes more effectively than words themselves.

There are five nonverbal abilities that are helpful to work on and pay attention to. These include:

1. Repetition - To reinforce what has already been said.
2. Contradiction - To contradict whatever the message is and make what you say seem untruthful at first.
3. Substitution - To replace words to create an effect.
4. Complementing - To give a compliment with a verbal message, like showing a thumbs up or patting yourself on the back.
5. Accenting - Underlining a specific part of the message you are delivering.

Body Language

Here's the thing. 60% of communication is nonverbal and gets delivered through body language, while 30% accounts for the tone of your voice. That means that 90% of what you are saying to the world is not coming out of your mouth. That is a dream come true for introverts. If they only knew. However, sometimes, you don't want to hear the truth. Even if you are not a good speaker, you can communicate effectively non-verbally. Although you have to communicate verbally at some point, if you can master non-verbal communication, you will do just fine. (The importance of non-verbal communication, 2015)

Have you ever wondered whether your body indicates something different than what you are saying? Perhaps it is displaying a mood that you are trying to hide, especially when something is bothering you. When you realize that more than half of the impact you make on people depends on your body language and not the words you speak, you tend to carry yourself differently. One thing the majority of people lack is awareness about themselves. Sometimes, people may have a thought or reminder to keep a good composure, but other times, it's not even given a second thought. There's no doubt that people who work in business or have serious and professional occupations know how to use their bodies to leave a good impression on the people they deal with or talk to. It is necessary to create a good impression when you deal with people that are considered important, or even employees and co-workers. The work you do plays a significant role in whether you have good or bad body language. If you put a lawyer who is suited up and strictly professional and put them next to a casually-dressed general tech guy, you will notice a big difference. There won't only be a difference in the clothes the two people wear, but there is likely to be a difference in posture, mannerisms, the presence or lack of eye contact the person makes, and the way they move. It, of course, is not always the case, but there are many body language mistakes people make when they don't have to be aware of how they present themselves.

Some people find it difficult to be on top of their verbal communication game, which is why tapping into non-verbal communication elements is perfect for coming across more confident. If you don't have control over the words you say, you can learn how to speak fluently with the help of your body language. It can be anything from adjusting your stance, gestures, and facial expressions, all of which are easily noticed in person and can't be filtered like we often do with technology. These elements are all significant when an audience watches you. Since you don't have a filter to hide behind, you'll have to try and get rid of your rough edges before you take the stage. While presenting your speech, you should strive to be positive, confident, and strong, which should be displayed by your body language. It is essential for helping you express yourself effectively, build credibility, and finally, connect with your listeners. It is especially important if it will be the first impression people will get from you. However, even if your first impression wasn't too good, it's still redeemable if people are willing to come back and watch you speak. By showing them you've improved, you will have earned the respect of your audience and be able to maintain a confident image going forward.

Effective body language will be able to support your strong image as a presenter speaking to more than just an audience, but also the world if that is your goal. Any audience responds best to speakers who not only speak with energy but also portray it in their bodies. This way, the message you deliver will be more meaningful, and your audience will support it because you are so believable delivering it.

Anybody who cares about what they are saying supports it with their body language. Whenever body language seems forced or a person lacks it in some way, they aren't likely to be respected as someone that has good body language.

Proper body language can be displayed with the help of:

- Gestures.

    These are performed with the use of your hands. How do you move them, and did you know that, when you fold your arms, you seem closed off to the people you are speaking to? That should not be the intention of your speech, and if it is a habit, you should become more aware of it and learn how not to do it. If you feel like doing it, try replacing it with better gestures. The same goes for putting your hands in your pockets. Again, this is not an inviting approach to your audience and should be avoided. Hands should also not be placed on your hips or held behind the back. Think of using them like the Italians do in everyday life, with passion, and to display meaning. They should be used to emphasize what you are saying and not be hidden. Hiding your hands is an indication of lacking confidence, which is what you don't want as this can make your audience uncomfortable. Your hand gestures should be big enough to embrace everyone in your audience, no matter how many people there are. It is also necessary to stand tall and instead of learning on an object, learn into the audience, to make them a part of your speech. It should seem like you are trying to shorten the distance that is between you and them. Some of the most effective gestures you can use will arise from the shoulders, so it's good to use your hands with your arms, and not focus too much on your wrists and elbows. Because the space between your hands and shoulders is longer, it indicates that you are closer to your audience. It can also make them feel like you are engaging with them, and like you are creating a comfortable atmosphere.

- Stances.

When you are speaking behind an altar, that's the only time you should be standing still during a speech. Standing in one place on stage or whatever platform it is you speak on, is very boring and can take away from the effective delivery of your speech. If you have an open space, move around frequently and try to look ready but comfortable at the same time whichever way you choose to stand. How you stand in front of your audience speaks far more than before you even begin to open your mouth. The stance you give indicates your emotions. It can tell your audience whether you are feeling happy, sad, angry, excited, and one of the most common feelings on stage, fearful. Even if you try and brush it off or cover it off, your audience will notice how you feel. That's why it's never a good idea to speak in front of an audience if you don't feel good. Psyching yourself up before a speech can be helpful to keep the energy going, and to help you maintain a good mood. The point of any speech is to deliver a message, but it should also be followed up with a good experience. You wouldn't want to watch someone give you advice or speak about something when you are interested in a bad mood, would you? No. You would probably wish that the speech was over.

Sometimes, putting yourself in your audience's shoes is a helpful way to check whether you are doing something wrong. By doing this, you can address it. If something about the way you portray yourself is offsetting to an audience, it should be to you too. You should care about what your audience wants and needs to see, and not just how you feel or think about your speech. Even if you are very nervous and struggle to move past it, it's necessary to try and make the audience's experience of your speech as pleasant as possible.

When you are standing, don't overthink. Keep a balanced stance with your weight evenly distributed, but almost slightly forward, as this allows for better engagement with your audience. Do not slump or lean on your one leg because it shows that you don't care. Your feet should point straight forward to your audience. Regarding the width, you shouldn't go past your shoulders. Your hands should be placed quietly at the sides of your body and project gestures with ease– not too slow, but not too fast either. Gestures can support moments of stillness or pauses to create effect. Don't move all the time either, as it distracts the audience from your speech. If you need to move, do so quietly and don't make any continuous movements, like tapping your legs or swaying your arms.

- Facial expressions.

The way you move your facial muscles, particularly your eyes and mouth, are all body movements you need to be aware of to build a powerful connection with your audience. If your words display confidence and surety about the topic you are talking about, then your facial expressions should support it. Proper eye focus is required to deliver proper engagement with those that you're speaking to. It is the number one part of your face that you need to be highly aware of, as it communicates sincerity, kindness, and credibility to the world. You can tell a lot about a person by looking at their eyes, and, so, it must always be soft, warm, and inviting, to indicate your appreciation and gratitude to have the privilege of speaking in front of an audience. Apart from your eyes, there is no other part of your face or body that connects as much. It's necessary to keep the focus on your eyes and not stare blankly at a point in the room.

To be an effective presenter, you need to engage with one person and then another and focus on them for a long enough period before moving on to the next. It can be done with pauses to boost attention and contribute to the comprehension of the message you are trying to convey. Other facial expression elements indicate your feelings, which can portray passion, concern, or anything in between. Keeping your facial composure and learning how to put on a poker face is good for winning over your audience before you even start to speak. Above all else, when you combine everything, you should be as natural as you can.

Although standing up in front of a big audience of people is never easy, with practice and consistency, you can make it more bearable. With proper body language, you can exceed the expectations of your audience, even when you are nervous.

Eye Contact

As a presenter speaking in front of people, your eyes are the windows to your soul. People can tell a lot from them, and apart from getting an idea about what your current mood or feelings are, they can also see whether your intentions are good or bad.

When you speak in front of people, it's your job to persuade your audience to recognize and potentially adopt the point of view you are suggesting to them. It requires you to deliver a meaningful, sustainable, and engaging speech, all of which should be indicated by your eyes. Maintaining positive eye contact will help keep your audience interested in what you are saying and will make them feel important as they are involved with the message you are delivering. Connecting with them properly by maintaining proper eye contact is helpful as you can connect with them on a deeper, more personal level.

The benefits of maintaining eye contact include:

- Creating a connection.

    The point of eye contact is to initiate a connection with audience members. That's why focusing on people in your audience individually is effective. You don't have to shift looking at specific people all the time, but you have to look at different parts of your audience to make everyone feel like they are included in what you are saying. It will make everybody feel like they are acknowledged. Deliberately looking people in the eyes isn't as odd as it may seem. Instead, it allows you a space to show audience members that see them and care about their thoughts. Sustaining eye contact welcomes an invitation to convert your use of words into a proper conversation. It helps create a bond between speakers and listeners, which makes the speaker speak with more ease and confidence because it reminds him or her of the purpose of why they are delivering a speech. It also makes the listener feel important and intrigued by the message that is being delivered. So, automatically, it increases their focus on the speaker too. When you maintain a connection, it helps to keep attention on you as the speaker as it makes people look back at you.

- Improving concentration.

    When you deliver a speech, a lot is going on all at once. Apart from the room full of people, there's also lighting, and sounds that can distract you. It is all very distracting, which is why keeping eye contact is beneficial for you. It improves your concentration and helps calm your nerves. By putting your mind at ease, you gain more clarity about what you want to say and deliver a more impactful message as a result thereof. Looking at people in the eye also allows you to slow down a bit and speak with more authority, which can gain you a lot more attention while it improves your focus and concentration.

- Displaying confidence.

    Focusing too much on what audience members do isn't always a good thing. It can make you very nervous, especially when it seems like they are not paying attention to you. The more you focus on this, the more you overthink. With eye contact, however, you can combat this. It doesn't matter what your audience does, as long as you maintain confidence, which is supported with the help of keeping eye contact. If you can do this successfully, you can communicate with poise and conviction, which will surely help you eliminate the distractions in your mind and get your audience's attention back to where it belongs for the duration of your speech. Overthinking is a silent killer of focus and can throw you completely off your game, which is why it must be controlled. The more you focus, the better chance you have of remaining calm and confident.

- Establishing engagement.

    Eye contact gives people the idea that you are there to share your knowledge and inspire them. By engaging with your audience, like asking them questions or making a joke at the audience's expense instead of just delivering information is very nice. Nobody wants to sit through a speech that is only packed with information. Instead, people want to experience something worthwhile. And, while you can only do so much with a speech, you can still create a positive and entertaining experience for those that took the time to come watch you. By moving your eyes among the crowd, you can see your audience members making different facial expressions, and perhaps even agree with you or clapping their hands. It is very good for the mind and can also help you get through your speech successfully without feeling too stressed. Whereas, if you look at the floor, your audience will feel closed off from you.

How to improve eye contact:

- Look at your audience first.

Think of your audience as individual listeners. Before you start speaking, take a moment to look at them and seek out friendly faces. Try to connect with the people in front of you and create the idea that you know what they want or need to hear. By establishing this, you can see whether it's necessary for you to brighten up their day or be constructive growth-wise. If you get an idea of what your audience not only wants to hear but needs to hear, you can make the speech all the more meaningful.

- Include people in your conversation.

Your speech shouldn't be too formal, regardless of what type of speech it is. It should be conversational and make people feel comfortable. Involving the audience in your conversation makes this possible. It's very impractical to speak without portraying a real meaning or connection, so maintain eye contact with everyone. It can be done successfully by dividing the audience into different sections and connecting with them individually as you scan through the sections with your eyes.

- Maintain eye contact. Not too little or too much.

Without making anyone feel uncomfortable, look at people in the eyes long enough to let them know you acknowledge them. It can be anywhere between five to ten seconds. Anything less than five seconds doesn't establish proper eye contact. Although it may seem like a long time, you can adjust it if you sense that people are starting to feel uncomfortable and then shift your focus to another person. It is also a helpful tool to adjust the rate you speak at.

- Work on your presentation.

Prepare what you want to say even more if you struggle to deliver your speech. Finding the right words to say can take away from your nervousness, which is directly displayed by your eyes. The better prepared you are, the more energy you can divert to talking and engaging with audience members.

- Keep eye contact with significant points.

At the points where you need to emphasize more, it is helpful to sustain eye contact. Wherever there are critical lines in your speech, ensure to stand still and maintain focus with people's eyes to make sure they are grasping what you are saying, and the importance thereof.

- Get to know your audience.

Although this isn't always possible, you can briefly acknowledge your audience members by meeting them before your speech. A great way to do this is to shake their hands and ask them how they are doing. Asking the audience questions during your speech makes them feel like you care and can make them feel more comfortable before you start digging into the deep stuff. Acknowledging people with the eyes altogether can also make them feel like you respect them, and thus creates mutual respect. Acknowledging different cultures without dividing them is also a great way to address a multicultural audience. With this, however, you should ensure you maintain respect and know how to talk to everybody on the same respectful level, culturally.

Movement

Body language isn't the only non-verbal form of communication you can use to impact an audience. You can also use movement.

We've already established that moving your body is essential to deliver a proper speech that makes an impact on the people who are watching you. How you move it plays a significant role in the portrayal of your confidence–something that any audience wants to see to continue listening to what you have to say. Since moving your body seems relatively simple to do, the act thereof usually gets neglected, and when you have reached this point, it can become quite challenging to focus on it. Moving your body intentionally but naturally should be your goal. You don't want to stand still on one spot when you deliver your presentation or speech, as this may indicate that you lack energy. You also don't want to move all the time, as it can seem disruptive or overwhelming to your audience. You want to move while remaining calm and still.

The effectiveness of using your body in the right way lies between not doing too little or overdoing it. There shouldn't be an extreme. Instead, you should find a balance between the two and only learn towards one or the other if you are trying to highlight a point. Body movement must be purposeful and compliment your message. It should be authentic and add a nice touch to the delivery of your speech.

Not to be confused, movement as a non-verbal communication element isn't the same as body language. You can't only learn how to do one effectively over the other. Movement can include upper and lower body movements and are practiced to be used in highly formal settings, speaking in places of worship, press conferences, political speeches, or any other situations where you don't have access to a microphone.

When you are presenting, body movement can be a helpful tool to support the message you are sharing with your audience, increase authenticity to deliver a natural speech, enable a balanced audience connection, and take charge of a stage. It is also beneficial for attracting your audience's attention, avoiding muscle stagnation, and steering clear from nervous energy successfully.

Just like there are body movements you should use, there are also movements that you should avoid when speaking. It includes:

- Pacing from one point to another.

    When you attend conferences, presentations, or watch anyone speaking publicly, you may have realized that some have poor habits, like pacing back and forth. It, like any other bad habit, should be avoided. If you imagine a ping-pong ball, when you look at it, it's quite distracting, right? Well, when you pace from one point to another, it's equally distracting, and believe it or not, watching you will become painful to the eyes of those that are. Any form of constant or repetitive movement is too distracting for an audience to focus on what you are saying.

- Swaying front to back.

    As with pacing back and forth, you should also avoid rocking from the front to the back. Any movement related to shifting our weight repetitively from the front to the back is also very distracting. However, unlike pacing, it can induce drowsiness in your audience. So, by doing this, you risk some people falling asleep, which is probably one of the worst things that can happen to you.

- Switching continuously between devices.

    When you are using devices, like a laptop and projecting screen, the last thing you should do is move between the devices too much. You can move from one point to another every now and again, but it is distracting, which is why you should limit your movement. If you know you are going to have to access your laptop regularly, then stay with your laptop. If you want to indicate certain things on the screen, you can use a laser pointer to do so. When you are working off of screens, be sure to make eye contact with the audience to see whether they are following you. When in doubt, ask them.

- Movements that could cause injury.

    When it comes to delivering a speech on stage, or anything else for that matter, you can only do too much to avoid falling. Apart from ensuring there are no objects in the way, you should know where the safe boundaries are on stage. If you do fall by any chance, you may feel humiliated and then distracted from your speech, which can also be disruptive for the delivery of your speech. Make sure you are wearing comfortable shoes, clothes that fit well and aren't hanging about for you to step on. It is necessary to study the stage before you walk onto it. It shouldn't be wet, slippery, or obstructive in any way.

- Clothing malfunctioning movements.

    Along with falling on stage, a clothing malfunction is something you want to avoid. Don't think it can't ever happen to you because it can. That's why you have to make sure you are dressed for the stage. If a stage is elevated, you should be cautious about wearing a skirt or a dress. The length of what you are wearing should preferably not go above your knee, and you should preferably wear a layer of clothing, like stockings underneath it to play it safe. You should also try and cover the chest area as much as you can. It's best not to wear a blouse with buttons. If you are wearing masculine clothing, ensure everything is well fitted and not too tight or obstructive. When it comes to clothes and shoes, you should be comfortable in every piece you wear.

- Distracting full-body movements.

    So, we've concluded that anything you do that seems even remotely obstructive must be avoided. Full-body movements are also very distracting. When you are on stage delivering a speech that you have worked on repetitively, you want to deliver it successfully. After all, the writing and delivery of a speech are nerve-wracking enough. The last thing you want is to distract your audience from what you are saying. When delivering your speech, keep your hand and upper body movements to a minimum, maintain a strong stance, proper movement, and adequate expressions to support your powerful speech.

How to add movement to your speech the right way:

- Move when you transition from different points.

    When you move around on stage, which is very helpful for delivering a speech, make graceful transitions using adequate movement. Moving from one point to the next present an opportunity to change the position of your body naturally, which is good as you don't want to appear too stiff in front of your audience. Stand firmly when you deliver your introduction, move your body with a transition to the first and second points. When you deliver a point, stand still with a strong stance, without moving too much between various points, and move your body to transition to the conclusion. When you deliver your conclusion, stand firm as with your introduction.

- Take steps forward when delivering key points.

Where you step and the direction towards which you step on stage has meaning. It can emphasize what you are saying and should be used wisely. If you form a habit of stepping forward on stage, it will seem like you are highlighting everything you are saying. It can take away from the primary points of your speech. When you lean forward, think of it as though you are about to say something of importance.

- Find the right position in front of the screen.

  If you are using a screen as part of your speech and you are presenting slides specifically, it helps to have your right or left hand as an indicator on the screen. If you stand in front of your screen, don't get in the way of what you are showing to your audience. Again, if you need to operate on your laptop, use a laser pointer instead to indicate on the displaying screen. Try to stand as close to the screen as you can, in case you want to make a transition from one to the other, but don't overdo it.

- Try to achieve a left-right balance.

  Every stage setup is similar but can be different when it comes to size, layout, or even the place you are speaking in. Delivering a speech is different indoors versus outdoors, while movement on a small platform differs from a large platform. When you are delivering your presentation on a screen, you are likely to stand on the left-hand side for the duration of the entire presentation. However, this may leave a portion of your audience on the far end right side feeling disconnected from you. To avoid this, try to find a balance between the left and right side of the audience by incorporating variety into your presentation. For instance, instead of only presenting on the left-hand side of a screen, transition halfway to the right-hand side. Although this may appear more challenging, it can help make everybody feel a part of the presentation.

  To incorporate proper movement and maintain a balance between the left and right side of an audience, you can map out various areas to add a range of activities. Some can be on the left side of the room and others on the right side. Whatever activities you have can be a part of the training you provide. It can be displayed with a whiteboard or chart that you can transition to.

- Use a prop.

  If you want to be more visual with the delivery of your speech, you can make use of one or two props, which can add some suspense to your speech. You can use it to build-up the information you share to a point of revealing the prop or use it to emphasize a point.

- Walk into or toward the audience.

    With training courses, you can walk around tables, chairs, or through aisles of the room when individual or group exercises are being performed. It will allow you to check the progress of those around you and can invite more questions to the audience space you are entering into.

- Distribute a handout.

    Adding a handout to your speech or presentation is a good idea, but when you distribute it, be sure not to overdo it. It can give you the perfect opportunity to move and engage with the audience but should be done without creating a distraction. For instance, instead of handing it out to each person yourself, you can leave a few copies at the end of each aisle for people to pick up as they walk in, or for them to remain seated, but pass it along to the members in their aisle.

- Make use of demonstrations.

    Demonstrations require full-body movements and can be used to raise the energy levels of the presentation. When you do a demonstration, it must be controlled and kept simple. It should also not take up too much of your energy as you still have to focus and get through the remainder of your speech. You can also act out scenes to add more effect to your speech.

- Pivot your body.

    Since some stories need dialogue, it can be ineffective when used in a speech, especially if it requires a lot of unnecessary or filler commentary. Although it is effective when carried out correctly, it can turn into a mess if done incorrectly. That's why you should be 100% sure about it and keep it simple when you do decide to incorporate it. If you are even slightly hesitant about what you have to say, then you should make it simpler or leave it altogether. If you are adding stories to your speech, you can pivot your body from left to right to indicate different speakers in the dialogue of the story.

- Sit.

    Just because you are delivering a formal speech does not mean you have to stand or move on stage for the entire duration thereof. You can also sit to take a break, especially if you are delivering a lengthy speech. Apart from taking a rest, you can also achieve certain benefits with it, like attracting your audience's attention, increasing authenticity, avoiding muscle cramps, and shifting away from nervous energy. It also allows you a chance to dial down your speech, take things slower, and breathe.

- Seek feedback.

    Delivering your speech is not only about getting through what you are trying to say, but it's also about learning whether your audience supports your message and the way you delivered it. Every so often during your speech, it helps to ask the audience whether they are still doing good or if something is distracting in the room to them. Gaining valuable feedback from your audience can help you do better with each presentation, and perhaps even improve the delivery of your current presentation.

Appearance

Society has always classified people based on the way they look, and particularly, dress. It's not a new thing, but today especially, it can reveal a lot about a person, and that is why it is taken so seriously. When you are a part of anything formal, like an event, speech, or even a status-associated job, you have to dress the part. If you don't, people will never take you seriously. It is relevant in public speaking. If you are delivering a political speech, you should opt for a suit with a tie. However, if you are delivering a speech in a more relaxed environment, this isn't particularly necessary. Nevertheless you should still clean up nicely for whatever speech you are delivering.

Of course, with public speaking, there will always be some form of judgment present, but as long as you know you've dressed and prepared for the part, you don't have to be worried. When you deliver a speech, you are presenting yourself to people. To show up in your best clothes and being well-groomed is an act of self-respect. You want to look your best when you are making an impact, right? Given that delivering any speech can leave a massive impact on people, you should be prepared accordingly.

What to address:

- Face and skin.

    Grooming yourself before a speech, apart from paying attention to your hair, you should also pay attention to your face and neck, as that is what your audience will be looking at. Men should always be clean-shaven or have their beards and mustaches trimmed. For both genders, noticeable blemishes should be covered up with cosmetics, even for men. Women should wear a natural face of makeup and not overdo it. Steer clear from distracting makeup, which means nothing too colorful or over the top.

- Hair.

    It doesn't matter what your hairstyle is, it should always be clean, combed or brushed, and groomed. If your hair is too long and tends to have a mind of its own, be sure to get a haircut to display healthy and maintained hair. If it's not necessary, place it behind your ears. Don't let it cover your face. It should also be free of dandruff or scalp conditions. When you wash it, it should be styled. If you feel that loose hair is going to distract or bother you, tie it up, even if you are a man. Regardless of what your gender is or how long your hair is, it should always be well-maintained and support a professional look when you deliver a speech.

- Hands and nails.

    Before a speech, you should trim your nails to a comfortable length, particularly men. Men should keep their nails short while women should keep it at a comfortable length. If nail polish is added to the nails, it should be light and simple like a clear or skin color. For women, nails should be kept simple. Long nails aren't very functional for a speech, and they can be interpreted in a wrong way by different kinds of people, so keep it classy.

- Mouth.

    Regardless if you've already brushed your teeth and flossed, it's necessary to also do it before your speech. It's helpful to carry mouthwash or breath mints with you to avoid having bad breath. Since you will be talking for a long time, you should take care accordingly.

- Clothing.

    Paying attention to what you wear is essential for the adequate delivery of any speech. You should look proper and wear something simple, pressed, and clean. If you do not have a suit, consider buying one and tailoring it for events like speeches. If the environment you are going to speak in is casual, you can dial down on the professional attire. However, you should still maintain a conservative look. Your audience will first perceive and judge you by the way you look before you speak, so it's necessary to look proper. Wearing good and neatly polished shoes is a must because even if you think nobody will pay attention to your feet, they will. As for accessories, keep it simple. You can wear a watch, your engagement or wedding ring, a matching belt, small earrings, and fine necklaces or bracelets. If you have additional piercings, remove it as they can be distracting. If you have tattoos, you should also cover it up as far as you can with clothing.

Chapter 4: Common Mistakes

Everybody makes mistakes. It's a normal thing that all people do. It doesn't matter what mistake you make in public speaking, it's how you deal with it after you make it that's important. Remember that making a mistake lasts as long as you allow it to. That is unless it offends someone in your audience. However, in most cases, it doesn't, and you can rectify it immediately. Even if you do by any chance, offend someone or get called out on stage, or even after your speech, an apology goes a long way.

Believe it or not, apologies aren't always something people know how to do, and you get individuals that are very prideful in these moments. However, when you do wrong or make a mistake, not owning up to it or acknowledging what you have done makes it even worse. It's almost worse to not take accountability for mistakes than it is making the mistake itself. Having faults and flaws are a part of being a human and should be treated as such. Of course, we can always do better, and every person is a work in progress, but only if they are willing to improve themselves.

Anybody who can look at a mistake as a means of growth in their career displays a lot about their character. When you welcome mistakes with the right attitude–a positive one–then, life gets easier and you grow. If you approach it negatively or associate it with incompetence or the inability to do something at all, you need to change the way you think about mistakes. It's a massive part of the growth process, and without it, nobody can develop into the best version of themselves.

Yes, it doesn't seem like that at the moment when you are on stage and trip over your words, say the wrong thing, or deliver a poor speech altogether, but every time you make mistakes, there are windows of opportunity that you can draw inspiration from. These windows will allow you the access you need to do better the next time you speak in front of people. By addressing every mistake, you are not just making a mistake, but you are addressing it constructively. With this, every time you make another, it will glide off your back and land in your pocket for you to work on later. It won't sit like this big problem, concern, or insecurity on your back anymore. Making mistakes can be rewarding. It can take you from novice to expert in no time. The catch is that you will always make mistakes. They will never go away. By working on them accordingly, you are merely deciding to deal with it until you become so good at dealing with it that it only aids in your growth–no longer your humiliation, fears, lack of confidence, or anything else related.

Mistakes are a blessing in disguise, and if you approach it right, you can rest assured that you are moving in the right direction. After all:

"The most valuable thing you can make is a mistake–you can't learn anything from being perfect."

- Adam Osborne

There are countless common mistakes in mistakes in public speaking because there is a lot of nervousness and stress related to the act of preparing and speaking in front of two to, sometimes hundreds or thousands of people. Of course, most public speakers won't speak in front of thousands of people. It is often only relevant for politicians and leaders, but a general number for most speakers is a couple of hundred, which is quite a lot. And, while you can't close your eyes when you speak in front of the masses, you should find comfort in the fact that so many people before you, and still today, struggle with nerves and fears about what could go wrong during their speech. Everyone walks on the stage with the same intention, which is to do the best they can, but if you are not there yet, it's okay.

Enough with beating yourself up.

Glossophobia is a fear of public speaking. It is among the most common phobias in the U.S. today. Keep that in mind. Also, be aware that 74% of people physically suffer from speech anxiety. (Smith J, 2016)

That's just more reason why there's no sense in pondering your mistakes. If so many people are scared of public speaking, then mistakes are almost expected. It's a new decade, and we can all learn from our mistakes, so instead of feeling sorry for yourself or throwing in the towel, let's.

What Are They?

1. Failing to personalize your message to the audience.

   When you talk about yourself, it's a given that many people won't like it. Not because they are not interested in you or what you are saying, but because most people like to hear what's relevant to them. Those who don't are usually great listeners, which sort of contradict a point of a speech. However, when you do the talking, even though nobody is talking directly to you, think of your speech as a message tailored to your audience. You cannot only talk about yourself. I mean, you can, but whatever you say must have a point or be relatable to your audience in some way or form. Speaking about yourself should be done to teach those who are watching you something or give them advice so that they can draw value from your speech. If what you say is pointless or doesn't mean anything to your audience, you can be sure that they won't return to listen to you again. You have to tailor your message–not to what people want to hear, but to accommodate their needs. They showed up to your speech for a reason. It's usually because of a need or desire to grow, improve, or be informed. By not talking to them about themselves, it's likely they won't listen. Public speaking is selfless in that manner. It's not about you. It is always about the people you are talking to, and to humble individuals that possess good intentions, it can be quite rewarding.

The mistake that speakers often make is getting the point of a speech wrong. Just because they talk about a past experience or anything relating to themselves, they can make it too much about themselves. With this, speakers usually lack other elements of their speech, like failing to deliver information or preparing it properly. Usually, when a speaker is unprepared, they tend to take it out on their audience due to their frustration, disappointment, or anger, which is something that must be avoided. If you've ever had this experience as a public speaker, you will know how bad it can be and negatively affect your credibility as a speaker.

2. Losing attention at the start.

   The introduction of your speech is very important. What you decide to say to your audience at this moment is sensitive. You should make it a habit of mastering your opening segment so that you can win over the attention and focus of your audience from the get-go. Curate it, make it interesting, highlight your goal with the speech you are about to deliver, and show the audience that you care. Don't ramble pointlessly, tell jokes, read, or apologize for anything. Present yourself as the confident person your audience expects you to be, but remain true to who you are as an individual. C. Instead, motivate them to be aware of what you are saying. You want them to listen, and they will if you make it clear that they are about to gain insight from your speech. Just don't be too verbal about it. Before you deliver a speech, think about what you want to say and start it off with a bang. Draw the audience in and keep them engaged. It can be done by telling a story that captures their attention, stating a statistic, or asking a question that makes them think or want to learn more.

3. Losing eye contact.

Eye contact is one of the best things you can have in the delivery of a speech because it establishes a sense of trust between you and the audience. It makes them feel like they can trust you, and then also trust what you are saying. When you look into someone's eyes, you can unveil them or draw up conclusions of them, which makes people feel like they are somehow in control of what they listen to. If they look into your eyes and you maintain a sincere approach to your speech and them, they will always welcome you. Many speakers can't keep their eyes locked with an audience. When you try and maintain eye contact, it doesn't mean that you have to keep it for the entire duration of your speech, but you do need to make an effort to focus on the audience. Since it is necessary to establish a connection between you and your audience, it is best to keep eye contact as much as you can and is comfortable for your audience. Failing to do this can result in a disinterest in your speech. By not maintaining eye contact, like many speakers, you aren't aware of how your audience is receiving your message or if they are still on track with what you are saying. There may even be points in your speech that people don't comprehend. If you made eye contact with them, you would know this and be able to elaborate on where it is required. If you don't maintain eye contact, you will continue with your speech, and the majority of your audience could likely miss the point of your message. A lack of eye contact also implies bad characteristics, like insecurities, arrogance, disinterest, insincerity, and detachment, which can be very offsetting to an audience.

4. Lacking energy.

When you do public speaking as part of your career or a permanent endeavor, you will be likely to speak a lot. It is the case for people who address large groups of people and are in charge of something big like a state, city, country, organization, and everything else in between. Over time, especially if you are delivering a speech repetitively or have to talk about a topic you don't believe in, it can be difficult to maintain adequate energy when you speak.

Nonetheless, without energy, your speech has no life and doesn't make an impact. The point of a speech is to impact people, usually to ignite an idea or change. So, if you don't have energy, you can't keep people's attention, and you will lose your audience. Your speech will become pointless. Energy is associated with authenticity and enthusiasm–two traits required to win over any audience. Without energy, you will also be perceived to be very boring, which is the case for anyone that walks onto a stage, whether it is an actor, performer, or a public speaker.

5. Being unprepared.

Nothing screams "I am not interested in what I am talking about" like being unprepared for a speech. Unfortunately, this occurs more often than people think.

"Failing to prepare means preparing to fail."

- Benjamin Franklin

And, still, most people don't prepare.

When people look at you and listen to you speak for the first time, it's a crazy experience because you have to be at your best. You don't have to be perfect. But, you have to show that you deserve to be listened to. If you are not prepared for your speech, your audience will get the short end of the stick and derive a conclusion about you that is likely to be negative. That's what you want to avoid. See, being nervous for a speech is acceptable, but only if you prepared adequately for it because the person who prepared for their speech tried to do their best. Even if they were shaky during the delivery of it, they still achieved much more than the person who was unprepared but confident. Such a person is likely to exude arrogance.

You are never too good to put in the work. You will never reach a level where it's not essential to prepare. If you don't care about your audience, what they take away from your speech, how they perceive it, or whether they felt good after you delivered it, then you shouldn't be a public speaker.

Remember that preparing isn't rehearsing. You prepare a speech to make sure you know what you want to say and how to elaborate on it where context is required, and questions are likely to build up to a point. You don't prepare a written speech line by line, and then, that's it. You have nothing else to say.

Don't rehearse. Care enough to prepare. Know the depth of what you want to say, not the words.

6. Using distracting movements or mannerisms.

We all make movements or misuse body language sometimes, especially when we are in deep thought or not paying attention to what we are doing. When you are on stage, however, you have to be self-aware. Doing too much or the wrong thing can be distracting to your audience. Body movement mistakes and mannerisms include gripping the lectern, playing with jewelry, licking your lips, touching your hair or face, fidgeting with a pen, and placing your hands in an unnatural position. Anyone who holds their arms looks uncomfortable or like they want to hide. The same goes for constantly touching the face. Biting nails is another big no-no that you have to be aware of avoiding when you are on stage. These habits can be difficult to avoid. The best way to address them is to change your habits altogether. Your goal should be to want to move purposefully on stage to maintain focus in the room you are speaking in.

7. Saying too much.

Don't be like the internet. There is too much going on. It is the very library of electronic information. You are not a library, and the point of a speech is not to dump data onto your audience. It's the same with rehearsing information, which you should avoid doing. It's good to have references in your speech–data you can refer to and rely on to prove statistics or expand on a topic. But, people are not coming to see you speak, download a Zip file with subfolders to store large pieces of information in their brains. No. Public speaking is all about the experience. If people wanted to research depression, for instance, they would Google it. If they wanted to learn how to deal with it hands-on or be inspired to self-improve and cure it, they would seek help from an inspiration and reliable source, like yourself with public speaking.

When you are writing your speech, there can be a lot of anxieties attached to what you are going to say. Will you have enough to talk about whatever topic it is you want to talk about? Or not? See. It is the part where speakers go crazy with search engines. It's a buildup of anxiety. There is nothing wrong to research more about what you want to say to gain perspective, but don't write it down to state facts in front of an audience. That is a big mistake. Public speaking is not the sharing of information. It is the sharing of logic, reasoning, analysis, and critical thinking with those interested to learn, develop, and thrive.

8. Saying nothing worthy at all.

Many public speakers are not inspiring, which can be quite disappointing to an audience. People want to be inspired, and when they are focused on development and growth, not being inspired by something they invested their time and money in is especially disappointing. To win people over, it's necessary to be inspiring. That's why it helps to integrate empathy, touch, imagination, color, sounds, humor, or other interesting elements in your presentation and speech. These are all right-brain activities that impact emotions that are vital for persuasion.

Since humans make decisions based on their emotions first before looking at facts or figures that justify it, it's necessary to make use of various tools to keep your audience intrigued and feeling the emotions you want to transcend to them. Using your words, visuals, and actions, you can inspire emotions in your audience. It includes hope, joy, surprise, love, excitement, vulnerability, and even negative feelings like fear, guilt, sadness, and envy. If you want to make an impact, you can strive towards being persuasive, engaging, memorable, and balanced with the information and inspiration you share. It's not wise to only focus on speaking to the logic of people. What's more impactful is to speak to the heart to ignite emotions in people.

9. Not pausing.

A bad habit of many public speakers is failing to pause during a speech. Integrating pauses can be stressful if you don't know how to do it. People are usually fearful about adding them into a speech as they are aware of the anxiety, time constraints, and adrenaline that comes with it. Most public speakers want to be prepared for everything. They want to be on point. The problem is that pauses can't be scheduled. You can think about it and think of where to put them, but you'll never know if it's going to be right unless you are in the moment. That's because public speaking is a live experience. Anything can occur or change at any time. Planning too much will not work, just like not planning at all won't, hence the anxiety or rush of adrenaline when you do see a gap to add a pause.

People take pauses very seriously, which is understandable. Most people want to avoid them as they fear making others feel uncomfortable or set an awkward tone for their speech. However, you can be smart with integrating pauses. Instead of avoiding them or making them as short as possible to get past your nerves, feel free to use them regularly but between transitions. For instance, if you are afraid of not knowing where to add a pause, consider adding it between slides of your presentation, after an introduction, or before a conclusion. Any part of the speech that has built up to a point deserves a pause before you tell your audience something memorably significant.

10. Overusing humor.

    If you don't know your audience or why they came to watch you speak, you should be careful with using humor in your speech. It can be difficult to know what's too little or too much, that's why you should only add it where you are certain it's appropriate. If you don't know your audience all that well, go easy on them. Telling a joke in your speech is fine, but telling more than one to people you don't know, can get awkward. Before you embark on a joke, make sure the audience is relaxed and inviting enough to welcome a joke. If the speech is about something serious and your audience is too determined to talk about that one topic or issue, leave the humor at bay. Getting your audience to laugh or even smile can be a real blessing and is a good way to break the ice. When you approach them with a joke, you must ensure you don't make the mistake of it falling flat.

11. Making excuses or apologies.

    If you are not feeling well, didn't get much sleep, stepped off a long flight, or worse, showed up late for your speech, instead of apologizing or making excuses for yourself, do something positive. Excuses and apologies to explain yourself may seem sincere and come from a good place, but it is quite negative, and even if you try, it's going to be difficult to explain it to your audience. They are there for you, and so you should show up the best you can. You can't help that you had a long flight or fell ill and don't feel like you lack energy, but you can make the best of what's still left of your speech. You will be lucky if you haven't missed a beat and feel a bit unwell.

Although it's good, to be honest with your audience, creating a sense of negativity underwhelms the expectation of your speech. So, rather than making excuses or apologizing, why not do the best you can with what you have at that moment?

12. Getting a Q & A wrong.

A Q & A helps fill up the time of your speech and shares even more insight with your audience. It is also a good way to get to know them and answer questions that many people may have. However, it's not a conclusion and should not be treated as such. You should treat it as a section in your speech. It's a part of the body of your speech, not what you close off with.

Think about it. Ending off with a Q & A means you'll answer questions until you get to the last one and then walk off stage. That's not going to be impactful whatsoever. What you should do is craft a closing section after a Q & A. So, still leave it for the end of your speech to ensure it doesn't disrupt the flow or message you are trying to deliver, but close off with a powerful brief that summarizes the key points or lessons from your speech. It should build up to a call-to-action and end with a powerful statement. Now, that is something people will remember.

How To Avoid Them

We refer to mistakes as common in public speaking because, well, that's what they are. They happen more frequently than people think. Those who are aware of this are likely to be afraid of public speaking as a result, while those who are unaware of it could be afraid of what could go wrong without realizing that it happens more than they think. As a result, it's almost normalized. Nobody wants to make mistakes, but if you make them, be kind to yourself. Welcome it like a pleasant stop along the way of fulfilling your speech.

When people make mistakes in public speaking, they are likely to consider why they did. They usually draw up the conclusions that they were underprepared, too self-aware about the opinion the audience had of them, or that they were too stuck in their head.

One can imagine how negative one of these thoughts can turn out to be. It can especially be harmful to overthinkers. If you have a good relationship with it in the first place, it won't feel so grave to deal with once you've made them.

It's all about:

1. Perspective - How you think of what you did.
2. Self-awareness - How you think and feel about yourself.
3. Resilience - The ability to get up and shake it off.
4. Forgiveness - Accepting it and moving on.

How to avoid common mistakes:

- Prepare, practice, and then practice some more.

    Don't prepare too much because sounding too natural makes it seem like you are unrelatable. If your audience can't relate to you, they will have a difficult time connecting to you and, as a result, lose interest in what you are saying. Being too perfect on stage is one of the main reasons why public speakers fail to deliver an impactful speech. On the flip side, don't fail to prepare either. Prepare enough, and then practice more, but don't feel like you should speak it perfectly. You can start preparing by writing your speech down a proper duration of time before you have to speak it. At least a week prior will give you enough time to ponder on it without overthinking it or forgetting what you've practiced. Once you've written down what you want to say and how you want to say it, practice speaking your speech alone. After that, practice speaking in front of an audience. People who have a greater fear of public speaking must practice it in front of people often before they take it to the grand stage.

    Public speaking is a skill, and just like you have to do it regularly to learn how to do it adequately, you have to do it repeatedly in front of others to fade out your fears.

    Whenever you feel nervous, your body is bound to enter fight-or-flight mode, which causes your heart rate to get elevated. It spikes adrenaline and cortisol and can lead to shaking, redness, sweatiness, and blackouts. The worst possible thing you can do is not knowing what you are going to say when you are in the middle of your speech.

    You should not be underprepared or overprepared, but you should not look for words when during your speech either.

- Keep in mind that the audience is rooting for you to succeed.

If your audience cares about what you say enough to come to see you speak, then they are routing for you to do well on stage. They support you, which is why you shouldn't be so scared. Of course, you will always get people that have conflicting questions and opinions that differ from yours. That's a part of being human beings. If you think about it, however, if your audience doesn't care about you making mistakes and they do want you to do well, they will be unfazed by mistakes if you can manage them properly. Make your mistakes. Handle them like a professional, and when you do, they will respect you even more for the fact that you do than worry about the mistake itself. People are likely to remember how you reacted to making a mistake more than the mistake you made.

- Don't get stuck in your head.

We have a lot of thoughts every day, which can turn into conversations. While you should think about the things you did during your speech and what you could do better, don't highlight what you did wrong in particular because you will focus on it for more than a moment. It will remain in your brain, and instead of letting it go, which is recommended if you want to excel in public speaking, people hold onto it. Sometimes they make themselves feel bad about it, other times they consider overthinking it a constructive mechanism to improve from it. Either way, thinking too much about what you did wrong, past a point that you can learn from it, is wrong. To avoid mistakes that are going to affect your speech negatively, look at your audience during your speech. Remain calm and see whether what you are saying resonates with them. If they seem bored, uninterested, or like they have a short attention span. Learn how to deal with that, not how to not make mistakes. Simultaneously, make mistakes gracefully, until it becomes a natural part of your speech that rolls off your back quickly so that you can continue with the remainder of your speech. How you deal with it is up to you.

Chapter 5: Your Speech

The process of delivering a speech can also be considered an act of performance. You are putting yourself and what you want to say–your opinion, thoughts, and feelings on display. It's impossible to hide what you feel when you are speaking verbally and non-verbally, on a platform or stage. Given that you get the chance to be impactful, you have an opportunity to make a difference and plant a seed in people's brains, even an entire society, if you are that fortunate.

What people say in front of others, and how they say it is significant. As you can imagine, if you are speaking in front of, let's say, one-hundred people. That's a lot of people that you are sharing your analogies or ideas with. It's not to be taken likely. It's a formal thing, even if it can be casual, depending on your audience or what you speak about. Most commonly, it is formal, and when you are speaking to a group of listeners, you are also directly speaking to each person in your audience.

Since public speaking is so impactful, it is looked at as a form of art that involves persuasion. You have to be persuasive in what you say to people because if you are not, nobody is going to take in anything you say. Nobody is going to think about it once you've said "thank you" at the end of your conclusion, and that's something you most certainly don't want. When you are a public speaker, you take it seriously because you have eyes on you. If you don't, people won't pay attention to you. You have to be enthralled in what you are passionate enough to share with the world to do so successfully. That's the only way you will become a success as a public speaker.

Now, given this, you can only imagine how crucial your speech is, so you best get it right.

If you understand public speaking and what it takes to deliver a great speech, it becomes easier to deliver a speech. If you are uninformed, you can't do the best of your ability. If public speaking is done correctly, it can have many purposes, which includes to inform, persuade, and entertain those you are speaking to. It can also be used to deliver a motivational, debating, or demonstrative agenda or idea, which people can learn from.

Public speaking benefits the speaker and the audience.

These benefits include:

- Personal development and communication skills.

    Speaker: The first time you deliver a speech publicly won't feel or look the same as the tenth time you deliver it. We are always evolving. Public speakers know a thing or two about growth. Let's just say that most have been around the block a couple of times. They know that the more you speak in front of others, the more you master your craft. Doing well in your job or something meaningful, public speaking for this matter, is addictive, and the more you do it and get a taste of what it's all about, the more you want to do your best, which requires you to grow. One thing you will particularly want to improve is your communication skills. When you do, you will realize how beneficial it is to communicate effectively. The more you learn to communicate effectively, the more confidence you gain, which is also essential to deliver your best speech yet. Confidence is directly related to self-assurance. If you are confident, you are sure about yourself, and when you reach that point, it becomes easy to speak your truth. It's more natural and believable. For your audience, public speaking is seen as a learning mechanism. It's something they invest time in to improve themselves. No matter what you speak about, they are there to listen to and learn something from you. So the better you are, the more likely they will listen to what you have to say, and who knows, perhaps even support you for a long time. If you are good, your audience will also be inspired to become better versions of themselves because they will see what it looks like as portrayed by you.

- Career and network growth.

Effective public speakers are creative, poised, professional, and have critical thinking and leadership skills. They are also highly professional. Anybody who has participated in public speaking or is trained in it, with practice, is likely to excel in their career because they are good in communication skills and can lead others. Anyone like this is very likable and approachable. They are also usually scouted by recruiters or companies and are almost always considered credible for exclusive roles. With public speaking, once you've spoken at a few events or delivered a couple of presentations, you are recognized by a lot of people that are prone to ask you for advice or admire you so much that they either talk about you or recommend you to others. It creates the opportunity to network with more people from different industries effectively, which can open a lot of doors for you professionally.

- Advanced critical thinking.

Speech delivery involves a lot of thinking. Even though you should not overthink it, you still need to be realistic and clear about what you are saying, which requires you to think about what you are saying. It is a positive way to grow your critical thinking skills. The more you deliver speeches, the more you will also think clearly about other things, including personal and professional decisions. Public speaking requires a lot of audience analysis. You have to think about everything that you are saying, from the introduction to the conclusion. You must be careful about what not to say or how to touch on sensitive subjects in a way that isn't disruptive, creates misconceptions, or negative judgment. When you are speaking with a room full of people, you are approaching the total number of people in the room's personalities, thoughts, and beliefs individually. Every person has different views and a unique way of thinking, so what you say and how you say it is crucial. You have to get it right. Over time, this becomes natural, even though it remains a challenge. With time, however, you learn how to deal with various situations effectively. You learn how to think in context.

- Establishing new social connections.

    With communication skills improving each time you deliver a speech in front of an audience, you can just imagine what it does for your social connections as you meet so many different people. When you practice, you learn how to approach people, have your opinion heard, how to debate a topic, and leave impressions, all of which allow you to develop sustainable social connections. When you are a public speaker, you are likely to run into the same people at different events quite often. When you make new connections, it's always a good idea to greet them when you see them again or show interest in their career as it can also create new opportunities for you to learn and expand your horizons in different fields. Social connections at events also lighten the seriousness of an event. Being acquainted with a couple of people can also be good for getting feedback about your speech, especially if they are in the same field as you.

- Personal satisfaction.

    Some people love the sound of their voice gracing the ears of hundreds of people, while most people loathe it. Speaking in front of people or even just speaking up and diverting attention to you is very stressful. It's a real phobia that many believe they can't overcome. When you have to do it regularly, every time you do it, you'll improve. You just have to get over the first few times, which seems a little extreme when you are in the moment and about to walk onto the stage. If you do feel overwhelmed, instead of thinking about how you feel now, think of how you will feel after—relieved and satisfied. To experience this, however, you have to give your best. It doesn't matter if you make mistakes. Doing your best is not about being perfect at all. It's about getting through your speech delivering the best you could at that moment, and doing so with your head held high. If you can just manage that, you will have delivered a successful speech, and that is very personally satisfying.

- Development of leadership skills.

Practice makes perfect, and if you've ever been worried about not knowing what to say or finding it difficult to express yourself, don't worry. These thoughts and feelings may seem permanent, but it's not. It fades just like fear, and a lack of confidence does. These are the things that keep us from our best or even first believing that we can excel at the successful delivery of a speech.

Most people who struggle to express themselves or talk publicly, even informally in front of people, don't believe that they have what it takes to improve and become good at speaking, especially in context. Instead of making their point of view heard, they choose to remain silent and keep their thoughts and ideas to themselves. As you can imagine, what they are doing is hiding their potential from the world.

If you don't speak, nobody will know what it is you want to say, and since we face so many issues in the world today, one can imagine that it's quite difficult if you feel like you can't express yourself or be opinionated about the things you believe in. Being a leader is all about having your voice heard. If you can make people listen to you and take note of what you are saying, potentially even learn from you, then you have become a leader. Public communication does that. It teaches you how to speak to people, many different ones. You get taught how to persuade, which is the key if you want to be heard. If you are interested in leadership and want to improve your skills, public speaking is the best way to develop yourself to get there.

Different Speeches

There are three types of speeches in public speaking, and each one of them has a purpose.

1. Informative.

    This type of speech is utilized to inform the audience about facts or lessons. Data that is backed up with research can be included in this type of speech. An informative speech can also have the purpose to explain how to do something. It can be a lecture, oral report, and even something as casual as teaching people how to cook or bake. It can also include an explanation of art forms, history, travel, and many other topics. Anything that requires more context can be considered an informative topic to talk about with this kind of speech.

When you choose a topic, you must ensure that it appeals to your audience members. Not only should it be dealt with at a level that allows for stimulation to share information that your audience may already know, but it must also be dealt with creatively. If the information you share is not stimulating, you will lose their interest and focus. If it is not creative, your audience will also become bored. You have to be an entertainer when you are on stage, even if you are delivering a professional speech. Choosing a topic relevant to their lives is also necessary to keep them engaged. If you are a painter, you don't want to listen to a speech about physics or accounting, but you sure would be interested in a speech about the history of art or like to learn how to create your own business and sell your art. Why? Because that is relevant to you. Physics or accounting? No.

We are all more interested in ourselves than others. We don't like to admit it but think about it. It's true, isn't it? That doesn't mean we aren't interested in other people at all. It merely means that we care about what we need. If you think about it clearly, it's not selfish. It's an act of self-respect, and although we don't like to share it, it's the truth. Public speakers should be aware of it as it helps deliver a speech. Writing an informative speech, think about how your specific audience will benefit from your speech. What will they learn, and will it appeal to them? Will they feel like they earned value from it, or not?

When you deliver this type of speech, be sure to have supporting material for your audience to comprehend the topic you are talking about. These include:

- Examples - This can be used to elaborate on what you've already said. Examples are often better understood than a chunk of information, so when you are explaining something, use an example to accommodate your audience.
- Facts - An informative speech needs facts–information verified as true and backed up by evidence. You should always include the source of your facts in your speech to prove them credible.
- Statistics - These may appear boring, but they are helpful, and while you shouldn't go overboard adding them to your speech, you can use them to add to the effect of an informative speech. To get this right, use statistics that are shocking or startling. It should add to the quality of your speech, not take away from it.
- Professional opinions - When you deliver an informative speech, there's no space for personal opinion. You can only use your opinion in a persuasive speech. So, if you feel like you want to share your point of view, opt for a persuasive speech instead. Delivering an informative speech means that you are exceptionally well informed about a topic. In this case, you share

expert advice with your audience, which is why they come to watch you speak.

2. Persuasive.

A persuasive speech is more personal than an informative speech. Nevertheless, it still has to be professional and requires a topic that can persuade an audience. When you construct a persuasive speech, you need to realize that people that are going to watch you could already have their own ideas and opinions about the topic and, as a result, may form an instant opinion on the introduction of your presentation. It can be disadvantageous to a speaker when he or she realizes that there are such people in their audience as it will be more difficult to persuade them–ultimately depleting the point of the speech.

When you choose a topic, it's important to take this into account. Pick a topic that you are passionate about because if you are not, your audience, especially the people that are acquainted with it, will notice. Passion usually shows in the delivery of your speech. Showing that you don't care about the topic is also very negative and can derail your speech.

To get and keep people's attention, a speaker will find it helpful to:

- Use descriptive language - To allow an audience to create clear mental imagery to keep an audience interested and entertained.
- Implement emotion - It is required to provoke an audience to care about what you are talking about. Without caring about a topic, your listeners won't remain focused enough to develop an opinion about it.
- Find an angle - For the topic you are speaking about, ensuring it hasn't been overly focused on or publicly talked about before. A good example is smoking cigarettes. Everybody already knows how bad it is for one's health, but people have stopped talking about it as a result. The worst thing you can do is to take a topic, like cigarette-smoking, and make a big speech out of it.

The point of your persuasive speech is to be convincing enough that your audience adopts a specific point of view, which is why a speaker must do proper research. When a speaker is informed, they will be more believable, which will show the audience that the speaker cares about what he is saying and how it impacts the audience.

To write a persuasive speech, you need an introduction, body of content, and conclusion. It can also include a Q & A section for your audience to gain more clarity on what you are sharing with them.

The introduction should grab people's attention, include a statement about the topic you are going to speak about, and a preview thereof to introduce the primary points of a speech. The body of content should introduce the topic in detail, explain your points or opinions by stating it, a reason for it, examples thereof, and restating the point. You should be as clear as you can to avoid confusing or misinforming your audience. A conclusion should consist of a speech summary and a call to action for them to ponder once your speech has been concluded. Everything should fit together like puzzle pieces and make sense.

3. Entertaining.

Speeches that are meant for entertainment purposes are used at weddings, casual events, and dinners. During this kind of speech, a speaker shares stories and makes jokes with a very relaxed approach. It's not serious and is meant to be enjoyed like any form of entertainment. The topics are light and sometimes funny. It serves a purpose, such as giving a toast or introducing somebody to a room of people.

When you deliver a speech with an introductory purpose, it should answer who you are as the speaker–only a brief overview–and what you will be discussing; what is the purpose of your speech?

With an introduction speech, you are presenting a speaker or performance, so you should keep it simple. The shorter it is, the better. With a welcoming speech, however, you are bringing people together to welcome somebody, possibly at work or at an organization. The purpose of this speech is to formally welcome somebody in front of others to create awareness about them. With this type of speech, you will tell the audience their name, their purpose, and give a small background about them–if it is appropriate. Entertaining speeches are also used for special occasions like award presentation speeches to present an award or gift. The first part of this type of speech will discuss the award, who sponsors it, the history of it, and what it takes to earn it, while the second part will discuss the winner and what they have accomplished to win the award. Finally, the toast speech is used at weddings and parties to praise or encourage whose event or celebration it is.

Getting Messages Across In Different Types of Speeches

1. Informative:

Delivering an effective informative speech, your preparation should include a series of clear personal and audience goals. These should have the purpose to enhance the comprehension of an audience, to maintain the interest of the audience, and to remember a speech well.

Establishing these goals, you should keep in mind that a goal is a result of what you attempt to achieve, which means that you should work hard and strategize accordingly to achieve them. The point of an informative speech is to communicate knowledge to people, so it should be the main end-goal that you strive to achieve. It has to be clear to you when you choose an informative speech. The more you get closer to reaching these goals, the better your speech will be until it turns into a successful one. When you practice this to deliver the best speech you can, the first thing you should consider is how to package an in-depth comprehension that you have cultivated of the topic. It can include research and personal experience, and be turned into a simple, communicable presentation for your audience. Another goal of a stellar speech is to make it memorable for your audience. They should remember what you said—not word for word, but what it taught them or at least the insight they gained from it. To ensure you are memorable, the delivery of informative speeches must include elements of repetition, organization, and focused visualizations with the purpose to boost the effectiveness of the speech that will leave the audience informed. Another way this can be done is to simply maintain interest from your audience, especially if you want them to return to watch you speak. If an informative speech can bring value to an audience, they will always come back for more.

2. Persuasive:

Some would argue that you need a type of specific personality to be able to persuade people, and although it is a convincing personality- sometimes manipulative—could get the job done faster, anybody can learn how to persuade an audience. With the right intentions in mind, you can get yourself there. With the delivery of a persuasive speech, the things you say are extremely significant because it will affect the people you are speaking to. It can potentially change the way they think, resonate, and create new ideas that they may believe in. So, what you choose to say is sensitive. It must be right, and to win your audience over it must equally be done smoothly.

When you are delivering a speech, you are attempting to persuade your audience to believe or do something, which means you should not only inform them about it. Instead, it should have a call to action on how to achieve it. You should also not complain about the topic. If something is bad, such as not exercising, don't just talk about how bad it is for you. Tell your audience how they can take action because they will be likely to appreciate a solution more as it provides an answer on how to solve problems.

To do this effectively, you should pay attention to who you are speaking to. Analyze your audience, and pick a format that is most likely to win them over. Always choose a problem-solution format. You should also place emphasis on the audience you are speaking to. The point of your speed is to persuade, right? So, you cannot try and get your speech done as fast as you can and fail to deliver a purpose. You need to make your audience feel as though you care about the opinions and needs they have. Think of it as talking to them and not at them.

It helps to build credibility in your introduction by making use of examples that they can resonate with, and then, of course, practicing enough without losing your passion. If they are aware that you care about them and that they take what they learn and turn it into action, then they will be more likely to follow through. It's much easier to act when you see that people care and believe in the thing you are trying to achieve than not having support or examples thereof at all.

3. Entertaining:

It is the most relaxed type of speech, but it is still crucial to deliver a good speech. You don't want the quality of it to be poor, especially since it's still in front of an audience. Since it has a purpose, to congratulate, toast, and present people or something to somebody, it's necessary that you get it right as you don't want to humiliate yourself and the person you are talking to, about, or presenting to.

The goal of an entertaining speech is to deliver a message in a happy, exciting, or amusing manner. The point of it is to connect with your audience emotionally and to keep everybody fully engaged in what you are saying or who you are talking of. To give an effective speech, you should be entertaining and make sure you don't bore people. That is why it is often a good idea to practice in front of somebody you trust to get an opinion before you deliver your speech.

You must hold on to your audience's attention for the entire speech, which can only be done if you set a proper tone and make everyone believe that you are excited to be there and present a speech. The tone should be so relaxed and well-executed that it transcends into your audience. They must feel as thrilled to be there as you are, and your speech must accomplish that. Keeping this in mind, you can't be in a bad mood when you deliver this type of speech as you won't be able to entertain people if you are not content to be where you are. To deliver the best entertaining speech possible, you must still pay attention to the structure of the speech. The audience must be engaged at all times, which can only be done if the speech is kept simple and brief. Time should be used as an advantage as you only have a short and specific amount of time to speak, which means you can keep it to the point and impactful. Like a persuasive speech, it should be memorable, and of course, entertaining.

If you are uncertain about how you can liven up your speech, consider integrating story angles into what you want to say. Start by saying something like:

- Why you should try something.
- What something means to you.
- Why you are grateful for something.
- Here's why you should do this.
- I had this one experience.

These are good ideas to add entertaining elements to your speech to achieve the goal of delivering a well-executed speech.

Controlling The Room

When on stage, there's a space where you will have an opportunity to capture the attention of your audience. If you don't manage to do this very early in your speech, then you are likely to start panicking, and if not, you have reason to worry. Refraining from the panic, rest assured that not captivating your audience from the point of your introduction or managing to control the room you are in, effectively, is something that happens to all of us. It takes skill to control a room and it is only effective if you manage to hold on to the audience's attention. Think of it as a basketball court with stripes to indicate where players can't move out of a specified area. Since you have a big audience, delivering a speech requires your audience to be fitted into this box, which can be done if they are interested in what you have to say. If they want to listen to you and find you captivating enough to remain focused on you, then they will stay within the borders and not move. However, if they don't, some will stay in the box, others will step on the borders, and then there will be people who step outside of them.

It will be complete chaos. Similarly, since controlling a room demands attention, people are likely to disrupt your speech by talking among one another if you fail to control the room. That's how you know that you are not impacting them as you should. Without attention, a speech is pointless. So, when you are on stage and attempting to get into a flow state where everything goes smoothly, what you should focus on is learning what your audience wants or expects from your speech or presentation. If you can't provide them with it, they will lose focus and interest, but if they hear what is relevant to them–

what they want or need to hear–you won't have a problem executing your speech successfully.

To own a room feels overwhelming terrifies most people, even those who excel at it. Just because you are getting it right or have obtained respect from the people in your audience, doesn't necessarily mean that your nerves will stay at bay. Delivering a speech can be mentally challenging. Whenever you feel like it controls you or that you can't get a hold on your audience and maintain attention in the room you are speaking in, try this:

1. Relate to the people watching you.

    If you are a public speaker, surely you've watched other speakers deliver a speech, so you know what it feels like when a speech is boring or so uninteresting that you would rather be anywhere else. Since you know this, these are the last things you want your audience to experience, so putting yourself in their shoes, you can understand what will work and what won't. It is also taught over time and doesn't become clear to you in one go. The more practice in front of a live audience, the more experience you'll gain, which will teach you what to do and what not to do. A speech should be worthy to watch, so if you could place yourself in the seats of your audience and feel good about what you see watching yourself, then you are on the right track. If you can't, then you have to put in the work to figure out what works for your audience.

2. Throw away the script.

    If you were about to do a live reading, you would have a book in front of you, but you are not. So, you don't need a script. Nothing you say should sound rehearsed. It should be as natural as the wind blowing through the leaves of the trees during the months of Autumn. Although it should be natural, every speech still requires a structure. The trick is to find a balance between the two. It should be a conversation delivered in a relaxed but professional way.

3. Make time for Q & A.

    Even though you are the one speaking, it's necessary to make time to listen to the people that came to see you. They are coming to experience you speak. It's not just a speech to them but an event, and when you allow them to speak and say or ask what's on their mind, you can gain even more clarity on what they need. By hearing their questions, you can deliver a centric speech that is narrowed down to what your audience needs. It is how you learn how to master knowing what they want to hear. It's how you realize what it is you have to say at the moment before you say it.

4. Stay human at all times.

   Compared to your audience members, you are on the same level as them. Just because you are the speaker doesn't place you on a higher platform or level as them. You feel the same things as they do and vice versa. You can relate to them and them to you. So, don't be afraid to get personal with them, while remaining professional, of course. You can meet them after your speech, shake their hands, and try to relate to their problems so that you can make them feel acknowledged and help them solve it. The last thing you should have is a superiority complex.

Having Self-Confidence

75% of adults suffer from the fear of public speaking, and when stress hormones are released, it makes people behave in ways that can appear unusual. It happens more frequently than most people think. You would imagine that people who sign up for public speaking have it all together, but that is indeed not the case. People who participate in public speaking are not always confident, but they are brave. These individuals like to learn. Some are afraid but do it anyway with ease, while others are afraid and feel like they want to disappear while they deliver their speech. They almost drag themself through a speech, and oftentimes, it's painful.

A lack of self-confidence is a serious thing. It doesn't only constrain you and hold you back, it can be quite awful and seem impossible to get past.

If you have natural self-confidence or can build on it to reach a point where you are not fazed by nerves, you will feel truly accomplished. It can be exceptionally beneficial for anyone who wants to do their best in every live or social encounter they have. For those who don't have the courtesy of this naturally, you have to work harder to achieve a good relationship with confidence.

It requires:

- Preparation and organization.

  Self-confidence requires structure. Being prepared and on top of your game with regards to staying organized is the only way you can increase your control over what could go wrong and how to prevent it. If you are not prepared, you won't even identify things that could potentially go wrong, which places you at a massive disadvantage. To prepare, you can visit the venue you will be speaking at, print materials needed a few days before your speech, create cards to use as cues, prepare for any technical faults, arrive early, and practice repeatedly to be assured.

- Managing nervousness.

    If you can get yourself to a point of dealing with your nerves appropriately, you will approach public speaking with a clearer mind. You won't have any anxiety, and as a result, you will feel comfortable and ready for action. When nerves disappear, you have a chance to perform at your best because all that will be left is your speech.

    To manage your nerves, avoid caffeine consumption before a speech as this makes you more nervous and can make you feel shaky. It's also helpful to implement mindfulness exercises, prepare a music playlist, and work on controlled breathing that you can implement before walking onto the stage. When you do this, you will recognize how unfazed by your nerves audience members are during your speech. By doing little things, you can look past your nervousness and focus on your speech.

- Positive mentality.

    A lack of self-confidence is usually caused by overthinking. When you think too much, you are prone to think of everything that could go wrong, which is not a good headspace to be caught up in. The more you think about everything that can go wrong, the less you think about what could go right. As a result, you may make mistakes that could have otherwise been avoided, and that will only contribute to a lack of self-esteem. To deliver your presentation confidently, you can practice meditation and imagine positive mental imagery about you delivering your speech, instead of pondering on the negativity that doesn't exist unless you allow it.

- Practice.

    If you can get yourself to a point where you are familiar with the content you are speaking about, the audience will be convinced that you are confident. So, even if you are not, you can sort of "fake it" to make them believe that you are. All you have to do is get your speech right. When you practice:

    - ☐ Stand up and speak loudly - the speech, transition, and the presenting of any visual aids.
    - ☐ Make sure you practice body language and gesturing for it to suit different parts of your speech.
    - ☐ Don't read through a presentation, deliver it like a performance you are proud of.

- [ ] Practice in front of people to get constructive feedback.
- [ ] Improvise and adjust your speech slightly for it to suit you, and for it to be received in the best possible way by your audience.

- Adequate body language.

If your body says you are confident, your audience won't be likely to see past it. You should use relaxed, slow, and positive body movements. It can include moving around on stage, maintaining eye contact, using gestures to emphasize points, matching facial expressions with what you say, reducing nervous habits, and breathing slowly, you can achieve a proper body language.

- Use nerves for energy.

Even though speeches are supposed to have a professional appeal to them, you can still emphasize your emotions. You can convey it to better express yourself. One thing you should not do is hide them. When you hide your feelings and mood from your audience, you lose confidence because you are focusing on hiding them and not your speech. When you display emotion appropriately, you hide your nerves, which can be beneficial for delivering a good speech.

- Address excuses.

Many people who lack self-confidence tend to hide from opportunities to speak their minds. They are often so scared of being judged or focused on that they try to avoid it as far as they possibly can. Some people say that their lack of ability to do something is due to their personalities or something they are not good at. However, by saying this, they accept it and use it as an excuse every time they are presented with a situation that makes them feel uncomfortable. Reaching this point can be quite difficult to deal with because the only way to deal with it effectively is to sit yourself down and address what's going on. You are likely afraid to deal with challenges and make excuses for them. It is the case for most people who lack confidence. When you have thoughts like these, they need to be addressed if you want to learn how to deal with them constructively. It can only be done by challenging your thoughts to learn how to communicate successfully, and then learn how to recognize how unrealistic most of your thoughts can be.

- Find a reason.

People who deliver public speeches didn't wake up one day and say, "I want to do the one thing that most of society hates to do, just because."

When you are a public speaker, it's a real job and must be something you are passionate about to do consistently, whether it's your primary career, a side job, or for charity. Whatever the reason is why you do it, you have to have a passion for it—a reason that makes you want to talk with people and inspire. Otherwise, you can't be good at it. When you find your reason—the thing that drives you to do it—it will be so important that even a lack of self-confidence will fade because it's simply too great and wonderful for you to mess up.

How To Write A Good Speech

1. Research the audience.

    Before you start writing your speech, make sure you do enough research about the people you will be delivering it to. It is the one part of your speech where you can't be unprepared. If you know your audience well, then you have a much better idea about what it is they need to hear. You will learn what resonates with them and can use it to your advantage. Be clear about what they need to hear, and you will have a better chance of persuading them and potentially entertaining them. By getting them to a point where they enjoy your speech, they will want to know more, and as a result, it will become easier to deliver it.

    When you research your audience, ask yourself these questions:

    - What does your audience need?
    - What problem can you solve for them?
    - What should you consider about your listeners?
    - What should you not mention?

    If you are speaking to a specific audience, meaning that they are coming to watch you to learn more about what you specialize in—like technology, business, entrepreneurship, marketing, or self-development—you will have to pay special attention to what your audience needs. However, you will have to research your audience before researching a topic.

2. Choose and research a topic.

    Once you've identified your audience, you can choose a topic to cover. It goes hand in hand with who your audience is, which will give you a better idea of what to talk about and how to do it. If you are going to talk about ideas or your business, in particular, you should:

    - Create a list of strengths of the idea or business.

- Compare your first list with the present or potential issues–this can be useful when talking about self-development too.
- Focus on areas where strengths meet needs. For instance, finding solutions for issues or struggles you may come across.

Something you need to keep in mind is whether your topic is intriguing enough to talk about. Consider choosing one that unveils a problem and highlights how to solve it, whether it's a self-development curve or how to improve a business strategy. It can be anything. When you give people the tools to solve problems, they will listen and want to learn more as many people who attend public speeches have the desire to learn and grow.

Just like you research your audience, you must investigate your topic exceptionally well. The more you know about what you are talking about, the more believable you will be. It will also aid in your ability to counteract mistakes or any issues you may have with confidence. Knowing what to say when you fall short helps deliver a complete speech because you never know when you will have to elaborate or say a little more than what you've planned for.

3. Write.

When you are clear about your audience and topic, it's time to put it all together on paper. Don't ever copy a speech or copy information directly from the internet or anywhere else. It's going to come back to bite you in some way, guaranteed!

Be original and as authentic as you possibly can. Once you've properly researched and studied your audience and topic.

Begin writing by:

- Starting with an outline.

    A speech needs organization. When your mind flows, it's great but that's not your speech quite yet. You need an outline to write a structured and organized speech that is adequate for your audience. When your thoughts are running, write everything down and keep it as side notes because your opinion about what you think is also essential to create a distinctive speech that focuses on how you perceive the topic.

- Be conversational.

    If the tone of your speech is not conversational, it is likely to sound like you are sharing information with your audience without adding a personal touch to it. When you write a speech, imagine talking to one of your co-workers or peers. Try and make your speech sound natural, but add different elements to it to make it sound interesting like a joke, sarcasm, or small talk. Remember that the best you can be is yourself. Don't try to put up an act in front of your audience. They will notice if you are being fake. Be authentically you, and they will appreciate the time spent watching your speech even more.

- Use speaker notes.

  Don't go and hold a full page of notes in front of you so that the audience can see it. Make little flashcards of thoughts or points in your speech. Don't write everything down because you will struggle to keep up with what you've written. If you have your whole speech in front of you word for word, you will also feel like you can't miss a beat and turn towards reading it instead of speaking it. A sizable page is a big no-no. Using flashcards with ideas or checkpoints in your speech is better because it reminds you of what you want to say next and elaborate on what you want to say more naturally. With this, you can create an authentic speech based on your preparation.

- Be 100% specific but engaging.

  It's helpful to add statistics to your speech, but don't overdo it. When you are sharing information with an audience, you have to be specific about it and provide statistics to back up your point instead of being vague about numbers or data. Using statistics or information backed up by facts is a helpful way to grab people's attention, so if you feel like the content you have requires reassurance, add a couple in there, and make sure you can back it up with more information.

- Keep sentences short and to the point.

  Since it's not smart to learn your speech word for word, make use of short sentences that you can remember and adjust effortlessly. Don't give yourself impossible things to memorize. Your speech should be simple and captivating. Nothing too long to make people feel bored. Using a variety of short and slightly longer sentences is also necessary for a powerful speech.

4. Pick a presentation tool.

It's helpful to add slides or a PowerPoint presentation to your speech. It makes it more memorable and captivating. When you do present something to your audience, make it look professional. Adding short video clips to a presentation for different sections of your speech or halfway also makes it seem like you've put thought into how you are going to present the speech. It indicates that you cared about making it more compelling or simplifying a topic for your audience. With the right presentation tool, you can add to an already-terrific speech.

5. Choose a template design.

    Once you've picked a presentation tool, you can decide how it should look. The more effort you put into it, the more your audience will appreciate it. A good template can make a big difference between an attractive, eye-catching presentation and something that is either dull or unoriginal. If you feel like you don't have the skills to make your presentation, you can hire a designer to create one. However, this may be pricey, so it helps to learn how to do it yourself. You can do this by using presentation templates from GraphicRiver or Envato Elements, to name just two examples.

Visuals

Sometimes, a speech by itself isn't good enough to deliver a proper speech to your audience. People appreciate visual effects, and since the average individual sees with their eyes first before listening, it's helpful to give them something fun or interesting to look at. Whatever you manage to put together should support your speech and add an element of curiosity to it.

Visuals can be a whiteboard used for demonstration, a digital presentation displayed on a projecting screen, or the use of props. Visual aids serve your presentation with a purpose. It adds meaning and thought to your presentation, and is used to help your audience get a better understanding of what you are saying. It's a supporting mechanism that contributes to your speech, so it shouldn't be used primarily. It should be implemented as an aid and not something to hide behind. Since many beginner speakers make the mistake of hiding behind it and implementing too much of it in their speech, it's best for novice speakers to keep to their speech rather than elements that contribute to it. Once you've mastered your speech, you can move on to adding visuals to support it and spark interest, clarify words, build emotional connections, and create abstract ideas.

Length Of The Speech

Some individuals may feel like they want to keep their speech as short as possible, and with the help of a Q & A section and the use of visuals, especially video clips, keeping the part where you speak short is possible. If you want to deliver a good speech, however, you need to take into account a good ratio between your speech and a Q & A section. If visuals take up too much time, they are too much for your speech. Again, they should support it, not replace the part that you speak.

When it comes to the length of your speech and figuring out how long it should be, it's something that you and you alone must determine. The audience that comes to see you speak is there to watch you, not somebody else, and therefore, you should take it easy. Take it slow, but keep it interesting. Don't feel like you have to rush because your audience wants you to get it over with. In that same breath, you shouldn't overstay your welcome either because the average individual's attention span is only that long. After a while, people need to get up, stretch their legs, and take time to process and remember what you've said. So, making it too long can also be detrimental. After a while of speaking it is no longer impactful, and you are wasting your and the audience members' time.

Depending on the type of speech you deliver, the length of it will differ. For instance, an informative speech will be much longer than an entertaining speech. Of course, the length of a speech isn't always up to you. Quite often, like when you are speaking at an event, it is determined by the people in charge, like the hosts thereof. When you are speaking with other speakers on the same day, your speech is likely to be an hour or less, but if you are delivering an informative speech to train people or educate them on a topic, it can be longer. Some speeches can even take an entire day, but this isn't the case for most speeches.

At the end of the day, it depends on what type of speech you are speaking and the purpose thereof, as well as if it's for yourself, like promoting or teaching, or for the benefit of a company, organization, or event. Unless you are given a timeframe, you should speak for the duration that your speech remains impactful and doesn't become boring. Once it becomes difficult to listen to, an earful due to the mass of information, or repetitive, it should be concluded. When you write your speech and determine the length of it, always consider your goal with it. The point should be to deliver an effective speech–nothing more and nothing less. So, if you feel like you can only be effective for five minutes, then that is the length of your speech, but if you have more to share, you can go on for as long as you feel it is acceptable.

The Beginning

Starting your speech, you want to be inviting and friendly. People who watch you speak must feel welcome and pleased to be in the room where you are delivering insight to them. You should not be awkward or make things seem uncomfortable whatsoever. The way you begin and how people perceive you at that moment is the way that people will think of you for the remainder of your speech. Some people get it right to change their audience members' minds if they've potentially messed up the introduction, but that's very unlikely and difficult to do. We all make mistakes, but try and keep your intro clean and execute it stunningly. It can only benefit the rest of your speech. Apart from being on top of your game at the start, interest your audience, and make sure you get their attention from the beginning. There are various ways to get your message across effectively, and it starts with a memorable introduction.

Methods to open your speech effectively:

- Begin with a quote.

    Choosing a relevant quote to the message you want to share with your audience members is a great way to start a speech as it gives you a ground to build on. Starting with a quote can inspire you to write the rest of your speech, and can also be used as something to refer back to when you conclude it. When you use it, be sure not to overuse it and ensure you reference it when you do use it.

- Say, "What if"

    Saying something that makes your audience wonder is a good way to grab the attention of an audience. If you ask a "what if" question, your audience will be curious to find out what you mean or the conclusion of what you and they wonder.

- Ask a question.

    The questions you ask in the introduction of your speech shouldn't be direct to your audience. They should be rhetorical or literal and act as another base of wonder for the members of your audience. The answers to your questions can be answered silently in the room by them. It can make them think deeper about the things you say during your speech by asking themselves the question repeatedly and deriving an answer as they gain insight into what you are trying to say.

- Say, "Imagine"

    Just like "what if," starting your speech with "imagine" can gain your audience's attention by allowing them to visualize a somewhat unpredictable or extraordinary scenario. It allows them to think beyond what they usually do and creates a window of excitement that they can ponder on. It makes the audience curious to know more.

- Be silent.

    It can be a pause before you start your speech, or saying a line or two and then remaining silent to create an effect. It can also act as a surprise to your audience as most audience members are used to speakers speaking immediately as they commence their speech. A pause will set the attention where you want it, which is directly on you. It will create interest that is only set on you and nothing else in the room.

- Make a statement.

    When you make a statement or state a phrase to catch your audience's attention, you keep them guessing until you reach the peak of your speech, which is usually toward the end of it. By adding a statement that makes them wonder throughout your speech, you win over their attention.

- State a statistic.

    Statistics must be relatable to your audience to get a message across to them in a simple way. It can trigger their emotional appeal, but to be effective, it must be a powerful, surprising, and personalized statistic.

The Body

While the introduction is considered a crucial part of a speech and the part needed to make an impact to hold on to people's attention, the body of a speech is just as necessary as it includes the center part of your speech. This part contains a lot of information that fills up your speech. Without it, there won't be anything but an empty shell.

The body of a speech is the most time-consuming process of writing a speech and specifically, requires an outline to break it down into smaller sections as it contains the biggest section of what you want to say, including key concepts and ideas. The body of your speech should consist of two to five main points. Any more than five and your audience won't remember them or the point that you're trying to make will get lost in all the information shared. Any less than that and you probably won't have a very strong or valid point, to begin with. Five points is also a big speech, so keep it to three or four if you can.

With the outline, keep the structure the same for each point. It should fit together like a presentation. Keeping it the same is necessary to help your audience follow the entire speech.

Principles of a body outline include the following:

- Coordination.

    It is the principle of topics being outlined into groups of information, thoughts, or ideas. It is balanced, and for each point, you require a group of thoughts that are similar for the audience to have a better time to follow the thoughts you want to share in your speech. Using coordination, you can construct your speech from the main points, break it down into smaller parts, and use the points highlighted from thoughts with the help of subordination.

- Subordination.

    It is a principle used for outlining topics that include different levels ranging from general thoughts to specific thoughts. The main goal of this principle is to highlight the main points and make them as specific as possible. It is done by pointing out primary objectives or points and breaking them down into smaller concepts and ideas that are simple, tactful, valuable, and interesting enough for the audience to understand.

With the help of coordination and subordination, you can choose the main topic of your speech and outline the body of your speech according to the main points you want to focus on in the speech. Then, breaking them down into smaller parts to talk about them in a greater context. It can be detailed in your outline. Consider it a skeleton of ideas that you are going to build on until you develop a worthy speech.

The Ending

Just like the beginning of your speech, the ending should be just as attention-grabbing. It should take everything you've said up until this point and remind your audience what to focus on when they think about what you have said. Since the purpose of a speech is to make an impact and sort of plant a seed in people's minds to think about, the conclusion is essential for this reason. It also closes off the entire speech and is necessary to bring everything to point so that you can highlight what you want your audience to take from what you've spoken about. You can also leave them with an afterthought like asking a question or ending with a quote to make them think about the message shared even more.

When you deliver the ending, you should be aware that people generally remember information better at the end of a speech than they recall it during one because they are constantly being fed with information during the speech. When you close it off, be sure to add a closing statement–something that motivates and empowers your audience to take action.

Endings are written to be compelling, which is the most helpful for creating a great conclusion. You can start with a story that maintains the attention of your audience. It can be personal or directed to the content presented in your speech. Adding this helps keep your audience interested. It can also include an experience or anything meaningful that will put everything that you've said into context. Creating empathy with your story is a good idea as it is received better by an audience. Secondly, you can add a surprising fact–something that can be interesting enough to re-engage people's attention. It can be added near the end of your conclusion. It always helps to add statistical numbers with facts to win over your audience. Depending on the goal you have with your speech, you can mention a clock and how we are running against time, and so we should not waste it and act before we regret what we didn't do in time. A concept like this is universally understood. We all have a life filled with years that will eventually run out, and so it is necessary to keep this in mind when we want to achieve our goals and dreams. It's a good way to convince people to act instead of wait, which most people today do. They are waiting for the perfect moment to start or feel good to try something new. Many people lack discipline. It holds them back from moving ahead and smashing their goals, so this is a great way to motivate your listeners to take the outcome of their lives into their own hands and turn it into something worthwhile that they are proud of.

In conclusion, you can also acknowledge people or organizations, focus on the central message if you want to keep your conclusion brief. If you want to use a visual element, you can opt for a summary slide as people tend to remember better with their eyes than their ears. Additionally, it helps to repeat a point you mentioned in the introduction of your speech. Finishing off with the key takeaway of your speech and being enthusiastic will be memorable for your audience to remember. As for asking questions, while the end of a speech may seem like the best part to add a Q & A section, add it as a section before your conclusion.

At the very end of your speech, make the call to action of your message clear to your audience, and thank them for their time to make sure they know you are finished with your speech.

Chapter 6: The Audience

Every speech requires an audience. Without it, there cannot be a public speech. When people show up for your speech, they come because they want to hear you speak and are interested in the message you have to say. Considering this, you must comprehend the type of people you are going to speak to because if you don't understand them, you won't know what it is that they need.

It's much like selling a product. If you create a product, the first thing you must keep in mind is who you are selling it to and what purpose it will serve. And, just like that, you have to consider your audience and the purpose of why you are delivering your speech. You have to think about how it will benefit them. If it doesn't, it is pointless because today, in the time we live in modern-day society, nobody wants to waste their time. With this in mind, just how will you get to a point to understand your audience well enough to know what they need?

Given that you will be doing most of the speaking and the audience will listen to you, what you decide to say requires careful consideration.

To figure out what your audience needs, you should implement these three rules:

1. Maintain an audience-centered approach when you speak.

    Just because you are doing all the talking does not mean your speech is about you. People listen to people that talk about them or something related to them more than they listen to people who talk about themselves. Public speaking is selfless in that way. Your audience is there for you to listen to you deliver a message that is relatable or directed to them, about them. Even though you are communicating throughout your entire speech, there is a limited amount of direct communication between you and the audience members. To prepare your speech, you have to focus on your audience and not only your message. It is an audience-centered approach typically used in public speaking.

    Getting to know who your audience depends on demographics, so you have to research who they are. You have to look at age, gender, education, religion, sexual orientation, culture, and race. Only with this information can you plan your message around the topic you've chosen to deliver to them. Your speech must be written with all the gathered information in mind.

2. Keep a clear perspective to find a common ground.

Offense and misinterpretation are everywhere around us. Society has become very sensitive, which isn't a negative thing, but it does require everybody to be careful about what they say, who they say it to, and how they say it. We can't just speak and think that there won't be consequences to what we say. There's always a chance, especially today, that something you say can be taken up the wrong way. For that reason, you need to consider your audience and maintain a clear perspective about who they are and what they care about. Don't be too opinionated about things you don't understand, and always be respectful about what you say or how you say it. By taking your audience's perspective into account, you can also reach a point of understanding them, and vice versa. You can use this to your advantage to adjust your message according to what they need.

3. Gather and interpret your information concisely.

With audience analysis, you can gather and interpret information through means of oral, visual, or written communication. With these methods, like handing out surveys to them before a speech, you can conduct an audience analysis. You can also interview a small group of audience members to gain knowledge about how they think or their attitudes towards questions you will answer in your speech. You can also use a Q & A section during your speech to interpret what your audience needs to hear in the speech that follows your current one. To find out whether your audience is pleased with your speech, you can always create a brief form that they can fill out to rate you, tick boxes of what they are interested to hear or learn about, struggles they may have, what their goals are, and how they think you can improve if necessary.

Analyzing Your Audience

When you analyze your audience, it helps you to identify them and by learning who they are, adapting your speech according to their interests, attitudes, beliefs, and level of understanding. If you don't study your audience, you won't be aware of what to say and what not to say. Since it's so crucial to maintain an audience-centered approach to improve your speech or presentation, you should spend adequate time analyzing them. In the beginning, this may seem quite challenging, but over time, you learn who your set audience members are and what they need.

You can use valuable tools to analyze them and adapt your speech according to what the audience wants to hear. Don't get it wrong. Learning about what they want to hear doesn't mean turning your words to the point that you change your entire message to dance according to the song they want to hear. Instead, it merely involves adapting guides to alter the content and stylistic decisions and routes that speakers make or choose to construct an effective speech or presentation. When you adapt it according to your audience's needs, there must be a fine line between over-doing and under-doing it. The distinction between the two, once mastered in a balanced manner, will be noticed and appreciated by your audience.

Factors to consider with audience analysis:

- Expectations.

    When you have an audience, you can be sure that they will come to see you with some form of expectation. By going against expectations or not meeting them, your speech will be impacted very negatively. With a speech, your audience expects to hear about a specific topic or gain value from it, so don't deviate from it.

- Audience size.

    Different elements affect a small audience than it does a big audience. The bigger it is, the more formal your speech should be. If it's smaller, it can be more relaxed. When you speak to ten people or less, sitting down, for instance, is appropriate, but any more than that, you have to stand up. When you are speaking to hundreds or thousands of people, you will need an elevated platform, microphone, and proper equipment to deliver your speech.

- The attitude of the topic.

    When you know the attitudes of your audience members about various topics, you can determine their goals, particularly the topic you are speaking about. You know that it interests them because they know what you are speaking about before they decide to come to see you. So, already, you should have an idea of what their goals are. You can get a clearer depiction of it by seeing how they respond to your speech and by looking at their answers during a Q & A section.

- Knowledge of the topic.

    It's always helpful to find out what the members of your audience's knowledge are about the topic you are covering before you write your speech. You shouldn't overestimate it, and even though your audience includes people who are well informed, along with complete novices, you should make it as valuable for everyone as you can. Everybody should be able to learn something from your speech. Tailoring it to what everyone needs can be quite difficult. Nevertheless, it can be done if you cover the overview and basic points of a topic and integrate interesting facts, stories, statistics, and opinions into your topic, you can meet your mark to leave an impact on every person in your audience.

- Setting.

    Where you deliver your speech can influence your ability to speak and your audience to listen. The set-up of the room must be adequate for your audience's needs, both in size and the arrangement thereof. The temperature, time, and internal and external noises must be taken into consideration. Then, there's also the type of space to consider, like whether it is inside or outside, if it echoes, requires a microphone, and if your audience will be comfortable in it. You should make sure you are aware of everything regarding the setting you are speaking in before the day of your speech. The earlier you can collect this information, the better you can prepare.

- Voluntariness.

    When audience members are prone to volunteering, it's a good sign as it indicates interest in what you are saying or doing. However, if they are involuntary, they are not as interested. If you can identify the difference, you can establish whether you need to adjust your speech and the delivery thereof. It can be a good indication of whether you need to adjust yourself or improve before you return to public speaking. Overall, it teaches you how to deliver the best speech you can, which can be measured repeatedly by checking whether your audience has a voluntary approach to your speech or not.

Chapter 7: Speech Versus Communication

Comparing your speech and the communication you deliver to your audience can be confusing because one is prone to thinking that it is the same thing. However, it's not. Speech delivery and communication delivery has a different effect when it comes to public speaking. It affects the audience in two distinct ways.

A speech is a mechanism you use to address your audience formally. Its purpose is to convince, persuade, inform, or inspire the people who are watching your speech. It has a lot of power when executed correctly and, in the past century, has made a significant impact on society and how we perceive human rights and freedom today. It has set the bar for how we live today, which is just one example of what a powerful speech can bring to the world. Without it, some of the most famous and pivoting moments in history, like freedom advocacy speeches fighting for equality, wouldn't exist.

The most famous and impactful one's includes:

- Elie Wiese, The perils of indifference in 1999.
- Martin Luther King, I have a dream speech in 1963.
- Harold Macmillan, The wind of change in 1960.
- Nelson Mandela, I am prepared to die in 1964.
- Eleanor Roosevelt, The struggle for human rights speech in 1948.
- Emmeline Pankhurst, Freedom, or death speech in 1913.

These figures are all remembered for what they said and how it affected people, and if you can do the same through speech delivery, you will have added value to the world. A speech is a tool of persuasion or information that can change the world, and while that's highly unlikely, you can still make a difference in how people think, the things they focus on and introduce new ideas and concepts that can change their minds for the better.

A speech's structure is simple and straight to the point, while communication in public speaking is diverse. It goes hand in hand with a speech and supports it to deliver effective public speaking. Communication is an act. It involves how you connect with your audience. Where you use a speech to deliver your concept, communication is implemented as a tool to support it. It helps you deliver your speech with feeling and meaning. It's what you do that makes your audience understand what you are saying and think about it accordingly. It's also what gets them to a point to take action. You can think of a speech as the structure you play off of to deliver a concept, but when it comes to communication, it's the platform you stand on. It's whatever you do to create engagement between what you are saying and how well your audience perceives it. If your speech is the structured message you work with, then communication is the carrier of it to deliver it in its desired form.

Chapter 8: Improving Memory

Remembering what you want to say when you deliver your speech all comes down to how you manage your nerves, because, if you can't, it can cause you to forget. Apart from forgetfulness, it can also cause a negative state of mind and induce your anxiety as a result of the idea of not being able to deliver your speech as you want to. The fear of making a mistake is linked to anxiety, and as you can imagine, if you can't remember what you want to say, it can make that fear even worse. It's also the same the other way around. If you have anxiety, your memory will be impaired.

So, to avoid this, you have to control your nerves, and believe it or not, there's not some magical way to do so. Instead, for the sake of delivering your speech properly and with confidence, there are three things you can focus on to improve your memory.

These include:

1. Repetition.

    Anxiety is often directly linked to a lack of preparation.

    "By failing to prepare you are preparing to fail."

    -Benjamin Franklin

    Repetition should be taken seriously when you are preparing for a speech because there is really, no other way of memorizing your speech than repeating it to yourself over and over again. You mustn't mistake repetition with rehearsing a speech. It is not the same thing and should not be treated as such.

    There is real power in repeating phrases and words in speeches or presentations, and when you are well rounded with a speech–when you know that you can remember it, that is the only way you can take what you've written word for word and expand on it even further. When you rehearse a speech, you will tend to learn what you have written. You aren't very likely to think beyond it because that will be your focus. You will only be fixated on what you know and be pleased with yourself accordingly. However, if you can manage to get past that, and elaborate to a greater scale that allows for effective communication, you can deliver a good speech. Repetition is essential, but only if you can use it to communicate with your audience. You can't take a speech, rehearse it, and then answer questions in the Q & A section adequately either, because if you don't have context, then you may as well be a robot reciting information to your audience. You are then, not a speaker, and you will make little to no impact. The purpose of proper speech delivery is to engage with your audience. They seek value from your speech, and so when it is embedded in your memory with repetition, you will gain a better comprehension of it, and so will your audience. Because, if you understand it, so will your audience.

How to use repetition:

- Point out the main ideas.

    It can be done before explaining them in context, in your speech. It can be done by prioritizing them from the most to least significant. Stating primary points, you avoid misleading your listeners.

- Show what's important.

    You can include stories or visuals to highlight primary points that will give your audience an in-depth understanding of those points. With the help of appropriate illustrations, you can do this successfully.

- Get rid of unnecessary points.

    Don't include unrelated information in your speech. Once you've listed the main ideas, remove any information that can confuse listeners. To get your message across, you don't need anything but the necessary information.

- Involve the audience.

    Be interactive with your audience and allow them to restate primary points or share ideas. It creates more interest for them to listen and pay attention to what you are teaching them. By showing that you value their presence, they will care more about what you say.

- Use different styles, humor, and visuals.

    The more creative you get, the better. Sometimes a speech can be very professional, but that doesn't mean that you have to hold back on adding a joke or visual effect here and there. At the end of the day we are all human, and making your speech more interesting, will only make your audience appreciate your efforts. Don't add too many details. Your message should always be clear and concise, but don't be boring either. By adding various elements, your speech becomes slightly more relaxed, which can also act as cues to help you remember what you want to say.

2. Speech focus.

Without focus, your audience can't pay proper attention to your speech, and they can't remember what you say. It's also the same for you. If you don't implement focus when you memorize your speech, you won't register what you are reading. When you memorize something, you have to comprehend it to remember it, so to memorize it, you require focus. You should not be distracted at this time and should learn it by yourself before you attempt to speak it in front of other people. When you are memorizing anything, you should also remember that you have a limited memory capacity, so if your mind is too full, you will likely forget what you've attempted to memorize.

To learn your speech, your mind must be clear and focused. On the day that you deliver it, you should not focus on anything else but your speech, you should make sure that you maintain a clear mind when you have to speak.

3. Giving yourself time.

   For every hundred words, you require at least an hour and a half of study. It may sound like too much time to study, but the general problem most people have while preparing for something is that they don't study enough. However, if you have a big speech to deliver, an hour and a half per hundred words do not seem as much. It needs to be embedded in your mind to the point that you can comprehend it. Spending so much time learning your speech may feel like a waste of time at first, but you must keep in mind that you will reap the benefits thereof once you nail it on stage.

   Keep in mind that you have a purpose when you spend so much time studying–to deliver the best speech you can and to rid yourself of anxiety and fear as a result of how well you know what you are going to speak about.

Chapter 9: Reading Your Speech

Reading your speech in front of an audience is a bad idea. There are several reasons why you should not do it, but first, your dignity. Delivering a speech should be like a performance. Again, it's not a rehearsal, and shouldn't be carried out as such either. If you ever consider reading a speech, remind yourself why it's not a good idea. It's unsustainable because everybody can read, and when you get on the stage to read your speech, that's all you are doing. It's nothing impressive.

When people pay to come to see you speak, reading is most definitely a no-go. They are coming to experience seeing you perform. On stage, you are live and in action. Your audience wants to be engaged, connected to your words, and feel included in the entire event. When you read your speech, they can't feel or do any of that. All you expect them to do is listen, which is not the way to go.

Valid reasons why not to read your speech:

- It is more difficult to execute a fine job at reading a speech than it is to perform it without reading. Even if you improvise with several notes throughout your speech, looking at the audience and engaging with them in what you say is still better than reading.
- Your script is like a safe hiding place. When you don't make eye contact with your audience, it seems like you don't care about them. It may even appear that you want to get your speech over and done with fast, which is not the message you want to send your audience.
- Not just anybody can read a script like it should be ready, meaning that not just anyone can read it and do a good job. It takes a lot of practice and proper training to be a good and impactful reader.
- Speeches are written in a formal language and if you read it, it sounds stiff, lacks excitement, and becomes boring, which makes it difficult for any audience to pay attention.
- By reading your speech, your audience will perceive their visit to see you speak as a waste of time. You could've just typed it in an email and sent it to them, which would suffice if you were going to read it anyway.
- When you read your speech, you are not communicating. You are just speaking what you have written, and so you will lack voice quality, energy with the use of different words, and body language, which will completely disengage you from your audience.

How To Deliver Your Prepared Speech

One is never naturally ready to deliver a speech, and everybody is prone to experiencing some nerves and self-doubt at some point in their public speaking career, but if you follow through and do the best you can, then you are the winner. You've not only made it to the finals, but you've won it too.

With preparation comes advantage, and when you've prepared well, consider the:

- Presentation format - Are you speaking alone or with a panel?
- Setting - Is it a formal or informal occasion?
- Audience expectations - What does your audience need and want to hear from you?

How to deliver your prepared speech in different ways:

1. Speak from your memory.

    To deliver a speech from your memory, you have to sound conversational and keep your audience's attention. If you can execute this flawlessly, you should choose to speak from your memory. Speaking from your memory requires preparation and practice. It is executed by memorizing your speech word for word and turning it into a stellar performance. Speaking from memory includes memorizing keywords to help you internalize a message. With enough time to prepare, you can commit to learning words that can be considered placeholders for what you want to say. To memorize your speech in this way, you can use your outline to remember a chronological structure when delivering your speech.

2. Work from your notes.

    Working from notes does not mean reading your speech, it just means that you get to look at a sentence or keyword to jog your memory or keep you on track with the order you want to deliver your speech in. It requires a balance between a conversational tone and formal structure. By working from your notes, you can feel comforted that you have something to support your speech, should you feel like you could forget something. This approach allows you the freedom to look at a script without looking at the entire thing to read from it. Working from your notes, you can prepare by starting with your script, dividing it into smaller parts or words that will trigger a memory, print your notes on notecards with large fonts, and ensure you number your cards to maintain the correct order. When you practice, you can place your notes on a table or stool to return to them in a subtle way when you are delivering your speech.

3. Follow your teleprompter.

By using a teleprompter, if you've memorized your whole speech, you can have the freedom to speak smoothly. However, reading from it can be very challenging as you need to keep up with scrolling through sentences. Using it can make it difficult to connect with your audience, yet it can be effective when used in high-stake moments. It is only the case when a connection with your audience isn't considered the most significant element of your speech and is preferred with a small audience.

When you prepare to speak from a teleprompter, you need to start by creating a bulleted list, outline, or script of your speech or presentation. You can mark a script with pauses, and ensure it fits the tempo of the teleprompter. Then you practice by walking on a verbal treadmill and keeping the pace. You have to remain on pace, otherwise, it will go too fast for you, or you will move too fast for it to keep up. To stay on pace, make sure you work with an operator to establish your pace, practice until you become in sync with the operator, and adjust the font size or panel height according to what's most comfortable for you. When you present your speech, arrive early to ensure your equipment is working and do a test run before you deliver your speech.

4. Speak from your script with 'holes.'

Having theories, hypotheses, or logic in your script as a part of your speech is a good idea to keep tabs on sections of your speech. These 'holes' don't have to be shocking or create a major effect on your audience, but it can surprise them or make them gasp. As long as it is interesting, you'll have a good chance of remembering it and can use it as markers in your speech to tie the rest of the content in it together. To prepare for a script with 'holes,' your entire script will stay intact, but writing it, you add the notes where you indicate the plan on straying away from the subject with a purpose. You can practice doing this by transitioning between what is scripted and what is extemporaneous sections. It makes your speech seem more interesting, and can easily capture your audience's attention when you've lost it.

Presenting your speech in this way, open it using formal text, and when you practice, indicate the holes you use by emphasizing them, work around them with the remaining content and you'll always have the attention of your audience locked in.

Chapter 10: Preparing For The Q&A Section

There are three steps to prepare for your Q & A section. Keep in mind that it should not be added before your conclusion. It's not the final part of a speech, as it's not memorable enough to finish off a speech. It's also not something you rush off. You have to make time for it and decide how many questions you will answer as you can't answer your entire audience's questions. When you answer them, you must be thorough and clear so that everybody's questions can be answered, even if you don't answer them from the people who didn't get the time to ask them. When you answer them, they must be informative enough to do so.

Don't be fooled in thinking that you don't have to prepare for this section. Not everybody knows how to answer questions smoothly, and since you can be presented with anything, you have to prepare answers for what you think your audience could potentially ask.

Prepare for the Q & A section with this strategy:

1. Think about and brainstorm questions.

    You won't always be on point with the questions your audience will ask, but even if you are not, you will come pretty close. By listing potential questions, you can gain context about a variety of possibilities and prepare for them accordingly. Brainstorm a list of possible questions, and ask your friends or co-workers what they would ask you about the topic you are speaking about after they've heard your speech. It is a good way to get an idea of what questions you should know how to answer.

2. Prepare answers.

    You can prepare answers to the questions you brainstorm, but you can't prepare precisely for those you don't know will get answers, but with variety, you will gain context on how to answer questions appropriately. Try and think of finding a common ground between you and your audience. By placing yourself in their shoes, you'll have a better idea of what they need to hear. Think of how your answer to their question can help them. If it's self-development or business-related, even better. You get to inspire people to become better versions of themselves, and so, you should present them with valuable answers. It shouldn't be recited, but you should know how to say what you want to say. It should be constructive, caring, specific, and meaningful.

3. Practice answering questions.

You have to practice answering people's questions if you are going to know how to deliver answers to questions you are unaware of. Only by practicing will you know how to talk to people and make them understand the answer. You also have to be able to comprehend the answer to a certain extent so that you can elaborate on it where it is necessary. Getting them to take action based on your answer should be one of your main goals.

Conclusion

To deliver a speech publicly is a real privilege. It's something that nobody can take away from you, especially, after you have delivered it. We don't get a lot of opportunities in this world to impact people at large, so when you do, you must grab it and make it worth it.

There are a lot of things that make public speaking seem fearful and scary. It's one of the biggest things people say they simply can't do based on thought and feeling. It's a barrier that so many people struggle to overcome, but they also make themselves believe that they can't do it. Is anxiety present in public speaking? Of course, it is. Can you do something about it and deliver the best speech to your potential? Of course, you can.

It's up to you. If you choose to limit yourself, it's a choice, just like deciding to try your best is voluntary. The biggest fear of all is not knowing what to do when you get up on that platform or stage. What will they say? How will you say it? What if you mess up? What if you fail to deliver? What if you are misunderstood? People don't like to fail. They don't like to make mistakes because it's embarrassing, but with the right approach and a decent perspective about how constructive failure can be, you can overcome your mind and barriers it presents you with. When you take your thoughts and feelings out of it, remove it from public speaking completely, what do you have?

You have your speech, the will, and the power to deliver it successfully. And, my, oh my, if you can learn the dos and don'ts of public speaking… If you can nail it like a top student, you can say what you want to say aloud with great poise.

The ball is in your court, and how the game ends, that is up to you.

References

Admin. (2019). *Four Types of Verbal Communication – MFLF*. maefahluang.org. http://maefahluang.org/?p=17

Articulation and Pronunciation: Public Speaking/Speech Communication. (n.d.). lumen.instructure.com. Retrieved September 13, 2020, from https://lumen.instructure.com/courses/218897/pages/linkedtext54276

Barnard, D. (2017, October 24). *Importance of Eye Contact during a Presentation*. virtualspeech.com; VirtualSpeech. https://virtualspeech.com/blog/importance-of-eye-contact-during-a-presentation

Benefits of Understanding Your Audience: Public Speaking/Speech Communication. (n.d.). lumen.instructure.com. https://lumen.instructure.com/courses/218897/pages/linkedtext54181

Body Language, facial expression, Public Speaking Skills. (n.d.). Totalcommunicator.Com. http://totalcommunicator.com/body_article.html

Body Movements□: Effective Public Speaking. (n.d.). English for Students. Retrieved September 15, 2020, from http://english-for-students.com/Body-Movements.html

Body Movement Tips for Public Speakers. (2018). dlugan.com. http://sixminutes.dlugan.com/body-movement-speaking/

Carpenter, B. (n.d.). *Demographic Audience Analysis for Public Speaking. Pen and the Pad*. Retrieved September 20, 2020, from https://penandthepad.com/facts-7663171-demographic-audience-analysis-public-speaking.html

Copyright. skillsyouneed.com 2011-2019. (2011). Verbal Communication Skills | SkillsYouNeed. skillsyouneed.com. https://skillsyouneed.com/ips/verbal-communication.html

Developing the Body of a Speech: Outline & Principles Video. (2020). Developing the Body of a Speech: Outline & Principles - Video & Lesson Transcript | study.com. Study.Com. https://study.com/academy/lesson/the-body-of-the-speech.html

Dialect and Vocal Variety: Public Speaking/Speech Communication. (n.d.). lumen.instructure.com. Retrieved September 14, 2020, from https://lumen.instructure.com/courses/218897/pages/linkedtext54277

Different Ways to End a Presentation or Speech. (n.d.). virtualspeech.com. https://virtualspeech.com/blog/different-ways-to-end-presentation-speech

Dom Barnard. (2018, September 6). *How to speak with confidence in public.* virtualspeech.com; VirtualSpeech. https://virtualspeech.com/blog/speak-with-confidence-in-public

Effective Informative Speaking | Boundless Communications. (n.d.). courses.lumenlearning.com. https://courses.lumenlearning.com/boundless-communications/chapter/effective-informative-speaking/

Effective Vocal Delivery | Boundless Communications. (n.d.). courses.lumenlearning.com. https://courses.lumenlearning.com/boundless-communications/chapter/effective-vocal-delivery/

Fear of public speaking: How can I overcome it? (2017). Mayo Clinic. https://mayoclinic.org/diseases-conditions/specific-phobias/expert-answers/fear-of-public-speaking/faq-20058416

Genard, G. (n.d.). *How to Be a High-Energy Speaker with Great Stage Presence.* genardmethod.com. Retrieved September 11, 2020, from https://genardmethod.com/blog/how-to-be-a-high-energy-speaker-with-great-stage-presence

How Long Should Your Speech Be? (2017, October 19). The Art of Presentation. https://timetomarket.co.uk/blog/public-speaking-2/how-long-should-your-speech-be/

How to analyze your audience public speaking - Google Search. (n.d.). google.com. Retrieved September 20, 2020, from https://google.com/search?client=firefox-b-d&q=how+to+analyze+your+audience+public+speaking

How To Deliver a Speech: You've Got Options. (2019, April 23). Throughline Group. https://throughlinegroup.com/2019/04/23/how-to-deliver-a-speech-youve-got-options/

Importance of Intonation in Public Speaking. (2019, March 5). Accent Reduction Training with LocalMasters | Learn American Accent. https://community.localmasters.com/importance-of-intonation-in-public-speaking/

Khoury, P. (2017, May 22). *Magnetic Speaking.* Magnetic Speaking. https://magneticspeaking.com/the-top-9-characteristics-of-effective-public-speakers/

Labianca, J., Oct. 04, R. comUpdated:, & 2018. (n.d.). *How to Be More Articulate: 8 Must-Follow Secrets to Improve Your Speech.* Reader's Digest. Retrieved September 14, 2020, from https://readersdigest.ca/health/healthy-living/how-to-be-more-articulate/

Memory Strategies: Public Speaking. (n.d.). universalclass.com. Retrieved September 20, 2020, from https://universalclass.com/articles/self-help/memory-strategies-public-speaking.htm

Memory tips to spark your public speaking. (n.d.). Buckley School of Public Speaking. Retrieved September 20, 2020, from https://buckleyschool.com/magazine/articles/memory-tips-to-spark-your-public-speaking/

Mitchell, O. (n.d.). *How to prepare for your Q&A session | Speaking about Presenting.* Retrieved September 20, 2020, from https://speakingaboutpresenting.com/audience/how-to-prepare-for-a-qa-session/

Noakes, C. (2011, July 14). *Reading a speech - 6 reasons why it's a bad idea.* Voice LTD. https://voiceltd.co.uk/2011/07/14/reading-a-speech/

Pronunciation Is An Aspect Of Verbal Communication English Language Essay. (n.d.). UKEssays.Com. Retrieved September 13, 2020, from https://ukessays.com/essays/english-language/pronunciation-is-an-aspect-of-verbal-communication-english-language-essay.php

PUBLIC SPEAKING ANXIETY | National Social Anxiety Center. (2016). National Social Anxiety Center. https://nationalsocialanxietycenter.com/social-anxiety/public-speaking-anxiety/

Public Speaking: Verbal☐: Biological Engineering Communication Lab. (n.d.). mitcommlab.mit.edu. Retrieved September 4, 2020, from https://mitcommlab.mit.edu/be/commkit/public-speaking-verbal/

Rehn, A. (2016, March 29). *Every Great Speaker Is a Fantastic Pauser — On Using Pauses and Silences in Public Speaking.* Medium. https://medium.com/the-art-of-keynoting/every-great-speaker-is-a-fantastic-pauser-on-using-pauses-and-silences-in-public-speaking-84b64f28f070

Role of Communication in Effective Public Speaking. (n.d.). managementstudyguide.com. https://managementstudyguide.com/role-of-communication-in-effective-public-speaking.htm

Scheltgen, J. (2017, September 6). *4 Ways to Own the Room During Your Next Presentation*. inc.com. https://inc.com/jordan-scheltgen/4-ways-to-own-the-room-during-your-next-presentati.html

Sergy, L. (2018, August 10). *How to get over making mistakes in your presentation*. Lauren Sergy. https://laurensergy.com/how-to-get-over-making-mistakes-in-your-presentation/

Sims Wyeth. (2014, June 18). *10 Reasons Eye Contact Is Everything in Public Speaking*. inc.com; Inc. https://inc.com/sims-wyeth/10-reasons-why-eye-contact-can-change-peoples-perception-of-you.html

Six Tips for Writing Successful Persuasive Speeches. (2017, January 30). UMHB Blog. https://blog.umhb.edu/six-tips-for-successful-persuasive-speeches/

Smith, J. (n.d.). *13 public speaking mistakes you don't want to make*. Business Insider. Retrieved September 17, 2020, from https://businessinsider.com/avoid-these-public-speaking-mistakes-2016-2?IR=T

Speaking, S. C. P. 7 E. in P. (2019, April 2). *SPEECH COMMUNICATION PROCESS: 7 Elements In Public Speaking*. Philippine News. https://philnews.ph/2019/04/02/speech-communication-process-7-elements-public-speaking/

Spencer, L. (2018, June 18). *What Is Public Speaking? & Why Is It Important?* Business Envato Tuts+. https://business.tutsplus.com/tutorials/what-is-public-speaking--cms-31255

The Importance of Personal Appearance. (n.d.). publicspeakingexpert.co.uk. Retrieved September 15, 2020, from http://publicspeakingexpert.co.uk/importanceofpersonalappearance.html

The most common public-speaking mistakes—and how to avoid them. (2016, April 11). Journal of Accountancy. https://journalofaccountancy.com

The Power of Pitch: Change Your Tone for Better Stress and Intonation in English • English with Kim. (2017, May 16). English with Kim. https://englishwithkim.com/pitch-tone-stress-intonation-english/

Types of Public Speaking • My Speech Class. (2017, May 2). My Speech Class. https://myspeechclass.com/speech-speaking-types.html

Uncategorized, in. (2016, November 28). *How to Avoid the Most Common Pitfalls of Public Speaking*. The Engaging Educator.

https://theengagingeducator.com/how-to-avoid-the-most-common-pitfalls-of-public-speaking/

Visual Aids: Effective Visual Aids | Public Speaking. (2011). Lumenlearning.Com. https://courses.lumenlearning.com/publicspeaking/chapter/chapter-13-effective-visual-aids/

Vocal Aspects of Delivery | Principles of Public Speaking. (n.d.). courses.lumenlearning.com. Retrieved September 14, 2020, from https://courses.lumenlearning.com/suny-publicspeakingprinciples/chapter/chapter-12-vocal-aspects-of-delivery/

What Is Public Speaking and Why Do I Need to Do It? - Video & Lesson Transcript | Study.com. (2019). Study.Com. https://study.com/academy/lesson/what-is-public-speaking-and-why-do-i-need-it.html

Zandan, N. (n.d.). The Power of Pause. quantifiedcommunications.com. Retrieved September 11, 2020, from https://quantifiedcommunications.com/blog/the-power-of-pause/

6 Key Tips For A Memorable Entertaining Speech + Topics. (2019, September 21). Ace the Presentation. https://www.acethepresentation.com/entertaining-speech-topics/

6 Steps to Becoming a More Energetic Public Speaker. (2014, March 25). Rob Biesenbach. https://robbiesenbach.com/6-steps-to-be-energetic-public-speaker/

7 Memorable Ways to Open a Speech or Presentation. (2015, April 2). YPO. https://www.ypo.org/2015/04/7-memorable-ways-to-open-a-speech-or-presentation/

www.ingramcontent.com/pod-product-compliance
Lightning Source LLC
Chambersburg PA
CBHW070419220526
45466CB00004B/1465